T0067198

MONSOON WOMAN

Wouldn't Take No for an Answer

LAXMI LALL

BALBOA.
PRESS

A DIVISION OF HAY HOUSE

Balboa Press books may be ordered through booksellers or by contacting:

Balboa Press
A Division of Hay House
1663 Liberty Drive
Bloomington, IN 47403
www.balboapress.com.au
1 (877) 407-4847

Print information available on the last page.

ISBN: 978-1-5043-1841-9 (sc)
ISBN: 978-1-5043-1842-6 (e)

Balboa Press rev. date: 07/17/2019

CONTENTS

ACKNOWLEDGEMENTS

It has taken me seven years and several revisions to write this book accompanied by much personal learning and many qualms and anxieties. That I was able to finish this book is because of the support and encouragement of so many people - to write truthfully and with feeling. They are my heroes.

I pay tribute to my daughter for her love and support which came with large doses of her incisive intelligence and insights; my partner who painstakingly encouraged me with comforting words and countless cups of tea over many years; my sister who talked to me regularly providing much needed love and impetus to carry on; a couple of dear friends (you know who you are) who read and edited my manuscript and made so many constructive comments; and my friendship groups and advocacy organisations for their unfailing support over the years.

I also thank the chief executive officers, directors and managers for whom I worked and who chose to believe in me. They mentored me, gave me opportunities to succeed and helped me on my arduous journey over obstacles to achieve end goals

Above all, I acknowledge my great debt to my parents and grandparents in this book. I have shared their remarkable stories, the values they inculcated in me and the influence they had on my character and the direction of my life.

I thank the many men and women who cheered me on, raised me up when I was down and continued to provide me with friendship and love. I salute you!

Without your unflagging support and friendship I could not have done this.

Laxmi Lall

13th June 2019

INTRODUCTION

When I started writing my story the advice I got was to write in a way that would not make it sound like an angry read. That people would not want to read my 'rants' against what they perceive as people's 'well-meaning' words, actions and behaviours. That I should stay away from commenting on experiences that were racist and sexist or highlight behaviour and biases that showed discrimination or stereotypical views. Nor should I mention words such as domestic violence and abuse or even control by religious patriarchal men. These words and ideologies had made many of my friends uncomfortable in the past and they wanted me to tone it down. They wanted me to play 'nice' and be politically correct.

I struggled to write it in a 'nice' way and gloss over the hurt I felt when I was dismissed or demeaned. However, I did not know how to write powerfully about something unless I had known and experienced it at a deep and visceral level. How did these experiences of violence, religious control, sexism and racism come hurtling at me after I moved from the society I grew up in, and became adrift in a new land. Each of these obstacles, in fact the whole series of obstacles were inter-connected and brought with them a range of powerful emotions. Therefore, I decided to write authentically about my own lived experiences, beginning with my earliest memories of what I was taught and observed as a child, the culture and traditions I was exposed to, then the moment of being uprooted from that familiarity and plunged into another country, society and customs, so alien to my own in many respects and yet containing many of the values and beliefs that were to become part of me.

This is my life. I have experienced both joy and sadness, love and hate, respect and degradation, riches and poverty, debasement and freedom. It is not inspired by anger but by passion: passion about my values and beliefs some of which were inculcated in me as a child and some I learnt as I encountered obstacles redolent with danger, control and abuse and overcame these to gain personal wins. As I look to the future I am passionate about bringing these abuses and violations to light in the hope of changing views and attitudes in order to make it a more equitable world for my daughter, my grandchildren and the generations of global citizens who are coming into their own

I do not believe I am a victim but a survivor and a winner. If I was a victim, I would have given up the struggle to free myself and find my voice and dignity a long time ago. I feel empowered and want to speak out. I have chosen to write my story using the lens of overt and subtle discrimination based on race, gender and age some of which have been wrapped up in domestic violence and religious control. My experiences are not new but they are my own. I do believe that most of the behaviours and words I write about are based on people's 'ignorance' of not knowing how others live and feel; of having been fed on images and stereotypes by various forms of media and versions of history written by 'colonising victors' or patriarchs, both religious and societal, about people living in other countries without having taken the time to understand or approach each person as a unique and wonderful human being

My story see-saws between experiences of condescension, discrimination, humiliation, derogatory comments, extreme control and abuse on one hand and kindness, help and support shown by some amazing people. It led me to come shining or stumbling through on my own.

I never was and still am not a superwoman who conquers mountains at a single bound. However, when I look back at my life I am amazed at my own resilience and stoicism which allowed me to keep smiling as I jumped over hurdles or circumvented obstacles in my path. I was not aware when I started my journey as a migrant to this wonderful country of the existence of glass ceilings or glass walls. All I had was a belief in myself - my knowledge and skills - and a powerful determination to win and survive.

I don't believe I am alone, just that I have chosen to write about it openly. I refuse to be blind to the topics of racism, sexism and misogyny and control in marriage and religion, which are like the proverbial elephant in the room. I refuse to skirt around the **–isms** – or the issues that have dogged me at every turn. I also recognise that not only was I transplanted to a new country but I was on the front-lines of a revolution by working women to be heard, get justice and treated as equals. There are many women like me whose voices have not been heard, who face obstacles such as violence and abuse, disparagement and belittling because of their gender, age or race, who lack education and opportunity to succeed. I can't tell you their stories but I can make you aware of my sisters, millions of women like me, who bear these burdens and violations of their identity and selfhood daily. Their time is coming as populations move countries and continents. We need to start understanding and changing our attitudes and ways of interacting with people of colour, ethnicity, gender identity, age and any sort of difference to ourselves. We need to open our hearts and minds and become truly inclusive and appreciative of all differences. That time is now - we need to call out and smash through the -isms – racism, sexism, ageism, domestic violence and control.

This is my story... a child born to privilege in the middle of the last century in India who embarked on a reluctant journey into an unknown land to become a woman of resistance, strength, courage and dignity despite the obstacles.

I have lived in one of the wealthiest countries in the developed world, namely Australia for forty-five years. I love my life in Australia and by this I mean not just the prosperity and career opportunities that I have had but the feeling of safety that I experience, my ability to aim as high as I can politically, economically, educationally and socially and not be pushed into being invisible or running away. Of course, there are barriers but these can be overcome or at least seem to be surmountable. Living in Australia has made me feel like a butterfly which has emerged from its chrysalis and set free to fly; however, it has been an arduous journey.

I came here from India, a seemingly third-world country or a less-developed country, in the nineteen seventies. But I was not a poor girl, a dear little thing who needed to be wide-eyed as she experienced the delights of the western world. I was born to affluent upper-middle class parents, who were liberated and emancipated in all sorts of ways. They gave me a private school education, all the worldly goods I needed, a university education, freedom to choose my own mate, freedom of speech and opinion that not many Indian women had experienced and freedom to travel internationally which even fewer Indian women had enjoyed in the nineteen sixties and seventies. I had enjoyed the upbringing of a 'princess', as someone once remarked, until I came to this wealthy, freedom-enjoying country, where I fell into an abyss of misery and pain, brought about by a combination of post-partum depression, migration-related trauma and domestic violence. This led me to a place where I was homeless and penniless or as one of my friends later remarked - 'left sitting in the gutter'. My story may not world-shaking but it is an account of relentlessly and determinedly moving mountain-like obstacles, stretching onwards and upwards, never taking no for an answer, and arriving at a place that I had not imagined I would be forty-five years ago – contented and at peace at the way my life has turned out: a feeling that I am reaching for the stars.

I am more than 'just another Australian'. I consider myself to be a citizen of the world. I believe my life experiences and this country have given me so much – resilience, strength and a good life. It has also allowed me to have the courage to be myself, to leave a situation of domestic violence, to speak up against racism, sexism and now ageism. I have also found friends in this land, both women and men, who have genuinely cared for and helped me, who made me understand my deep inner strengths and empowered me to act and speak with courage and dignity.

At the same time, living in the free and developed world has also posed constant challenges. Despite my beliefs about the freedom and egalitarianism of the western world, I have experienced racism, sexism and ageism which when compounded with the sadism experienced in domestic violence to become a 'quadruple whammy'. After years of assimilation and fitting in, I am tired of still being described as a dark-skinned woman from an eastern background and asked by newly introduced people for my favourite curry recipe. I am tired of being asked at interviews, events, parties and just walking in the park 'Where are you from?' – as if people are blind to the fact that I am from a South Asian background.

To tell you the truth, I am at times bewildered but 'not at all amused' when the richness of my identity is evident but so many seem blind to it. They choose to see me as a package of brown stuff. Their curiosity trumps their sensitivity to my feelings!

In anger and sometimes despair, I bark a reply 'Timbuktoo' or the name of the suburb I live in. And when they persist, 'But before that', I reel off names of the suburbs and cities I have lived in until I finally say with exasperation, 'my mother's womb'! By their singular insistence, they are really saying : 'You are not an Australian' implying 'you are not white like us'. Some of them rationalise by saying they are curious but I wonder if it is their lack of sophistication or an understanding of privacy when they ask their wide-eyed question. The practice continues despite the fact that Australia, apart from its Indigenous peoples, is made up of migrants of all shades – white, black, brown, tan, yellow, brindle. I am tired of being confronted with this relentless intrusion into my ethnicity. I wonder with sadness why people don't choose to be kind and friendly before they plunge into satisfying their curiosity. I am tired of feeling excluded because of the colour of my skin.

This current of unconscious racism is not restricted to Australia. I recently read an American journalist, who said that being interrogated about one's background is a kind of ordinary racism that Americans of Asian, Middle-eastern or other origins often have to face though I would argue that this applies to almost all people of different ethnic backgrounds. He was commenting on a news report where the CEO of a large organisation, interrupted a professional analyst's summing up of a dangerous world situation to ask her, 'Where are you from?' Her answer that she was from one of the largest cities in USA did not satisfy him. He continued to prod till she eventually said her parents had come from an Asian country. The implication, of course, is that children of Asian immigrants can never truly be 'from' America (or Australia or a European nation) and feels like a rejection of the classic 'melting pot' ideal. This blatant sexism and racism reduced a professional woman to being known by her physical appearance and gender.

Referring to people's relentlessly curious questions: I heard some wonderful poetry recently by someone who described his life's journey in coming to terms with his vulnerable true self including his homelessness and transitioning his gender. Some words from his poem stole my heart as it resonated with what I have been feeling and saying about being relentlessly questioned at a first meeting before the word hello is out of my mouth. His powerful poem asked people to cease asking him as to when he knew he wanted to change his gender because they didn't need to know what had happened in the past or when he started to having various body parts operated on. Instead they needed to get to know him as a friend over a cup of coffee, thus establishing a relationship of trust and affection before questioning him regarding the details of his gender change or accompanying inner emotional conflicts.

Similar sentiments are expressed by a writer of middle-eastern origin who lives in USA. He says on the subject of intrusive personal questions from people who meet him for the first time; he knows what they mean and realises that almost never have any real malice in mind. It's just that their curiosity has been sparked by his skin colour and name. Like many other migrants I too resent this intrusive questioning which seeks to put a label on me; it implies that my identity is determined by my skin and ethnicity something over which I had no choice and have no power to change. All I want to say: I am more than my skin colour and place of ethnic origin.

Like the millions of people who have migrated to the USA, UK, Canada, Europe or Australia, I have a hyphenated identity. 'Left of the hyphen, I'm a person of south Asian origin. But that's not all that I am'. In fact, it is an infinitesimal part of who I am.

OVERCOMING BARRIERS AND BECOMING ME

To those of you who are interested in knowing who I am right of the hyphen: I describe myself as a writer, educator and commentator, social activist, a fluent speaker of three languages (plus a smattering of two others). I am also a mother, good friend to many, an Australian citizen, a lover of western and eastern literature, a reader of history (ancient and medieval) and crime fiction of all genres particularly Nordic noire, doer of cryptic crosswords and brain-games, lover of scrabble, a hater of injustice, a world-traveller and a frequent flyer, a designer and creator of women's clothes, textile-art and costume jewellery, a lover of comedy who secretly longs to be a stand-up comic, interested in all aspects of international geo-political news, active in women's affairs including domestic violence, pay equity and raising the status of women of multi-cultural identities and also someone who has struggled with existential angst for many years. So when people ask me that dreadful question - 'Where are you from?' to satisfy their own boundless curiosity, it may help them to locate my ethnicity but it will never describe me in my entirety.

I am also a transplant – perhaps exotic or endangered. I was born in another country and was transplanted to Australia when I was twenty-five years old. I came as an adult with the feelings, beliefs and reactions derived from my childhood and upbringing. However, forty-five years later I have imbibed and am now steeped in western culture and Australia's customs, values, socio- political and work mores. The western-brand of feminism which I first discovered in the late nineteen seventies and early nineteen eighties has sent deep taproots into my soul. But, I think of myself as a proud feminist and a citizen of the world because of my adult experiences and the values that have formed me.

My challenging experiences have led me to morph into a woman with strong views about identity and individuality. It has led me to becoming a fully-grown feminist. My conversion to feminism was slow in maturing and may be called accidental; however, my life experiences lead me to believe that I am an intersectional feminist. ' Intersectionality' has only recently been added to various dictionaries and it means more than just the intersection of race and gender. One way to define 'intersectionality' is to say it includes *any* kind of discrimination whether based on gender, race, age, class, socioeconomic status, physical or mental ability, gender or sexual identity, religion, or ethnicity.

All of this seems to bypass the consciousness of many westerners including many Australians – all they see is a dark-skinned, older woman who could not possibly know as much as they do... not a 'fair dinkum (or real) Aussie'. I am left thinking that their mental image of a genuine Australian is a lithe, fair-skinned blonde with northern European looks.

Many people I come across show their ignorance and woeful insularity. In recent times, I have had two sorts of interactions from white people who don't know me. I have three sorts of effects on people who meet me for the first time: either they charge up and ask 'Where are you from?' trying to place my 'exotic looks'; or their eyes glaze over and pass over me if I am part of a larger group: or they take over the conversation and 'mansplain' or 'womansplain' some basic tenets of life and/or current affairs prevalent in western society. I have to shake myself and silently ask if I look stupid or half-witted. Such people never bother to enquire if I have heard of this or that before? I don't think they take into account my command of English language, an excellent education and wide knowledge, and a large repertoire of emotional skills. I believe these qualities of language, knowledge and education are instantly knowable when we talk to someone. Perhaps, they believe 'white' is synonymous with superiority, currency of knowledge and expertise in all things global and local. At one end of the spectrum, I experience patronising behaviour which grows almost exponentially to become humiliation, hurt, abuse and outright discrimination at the other end of the spectrum. The underlying vein of indirect, unconscious discrimination flows quietly along the fault lines of systemic discrimination or unconscious bias which is so rife in many areas of white society. Some have called it 'benevolent racism' and so it may be – unconscious racism or exclusion masked by conscious patronage.

The conclusions I have drawn about ignorance and insularity and the expressions and words used by white people when confronted by the existence of structural racism are echoed by many writers and commentators who exist on the other side of the 'white' skin divide. These are 'black' writers and other ethnicities who comment on the huge gulf of emotional disconnection displayed by white people when a black/brown/person of colour articulates their experiences. I have seen the shutters fall over their eyes, their facial expressions harden. It almost seems that their ears are filled with 'treacle' and they are indifferent to our words.

Similar thoughts are articulated in various articles on the topic of 'white Privilege', many of which are freely available on the internet. White people seem to have no idea how people of colour (of all shades) live with the constant day-in-day-out discrimination, which makes them feel like an 'other'. The focus is on their external looks, their hair, nose, eyes, body shape, clothes, food from their country of origin. When you bring it to their attention they deny that they are being patronising or discriminatory. However, discrimination is rife in our society both above the line and below the line. And when you say that questioning people about their country of origin, they say they are curious but they don't seem to understand how unconsciously racist it is.

I got a glimpse of the sub-strata of conscious and unconscious racism at a recent seminar conducted by anti-racist educator who spoke about the defensive attitude (which she calls 'fragility') adopted by white people when shown how their words and behaviour which offend and hurt people of colour. The educator commented that the defensiveness is lit by emotions such as anger, fear and guilt among other behaviours. In fact, she said, racism as a practice is not restricted to "bad people". It is embedded in the deep structures and systems of our society.

Like many authors on this subject, I am struck with the unconscious behaviour and bias of many of my colleagues and acquaintances; they see no need to inform or educate themselves regarding social issues and sensitivities and instead defend their behaviours and words. When I ask them why they want to know where I am from, they mumble 'Because I like to know people's ethnicity', or 'I like your type of food', or as one woman put it 'I think it's okay because it is a well-intentioned question'. There is no hint of empathy nor understanding in their words even when reminded that the question is tiresome for people who have been asked that hundreds of times. I say 'walk a mile in my shoes' to really understand how trite and prying you sound. Such words and behaviours are woefully ignorant and socially insensitive at best and unconsciously racist at the worst.

I know that culture and mores are constructed a little at a time by the people who live in a society or microcosm. They do not appear all of a sudden on their own. Australia like USA or Canada or the UK is a mix, a hotchpotch or minestrone soup of the people who have lived there for centuries as well as the newcomers who have arrived over the past fifty or a hundred years. The greatest migrations in human history have taken place over the past hundred years. Most of the modern 'developed' world seems to be composed of migrants, both willing and unwilling, some wanting to be immersed in the new, 'civilised' culture and those wanting to stay apart. These migrants have contributed to making their new countries strong, resilient and economically prosperous as they are today.

Like these economically developed countries, people of colour like me have been metamorphosing over the years. I am an artefact of the modern world, that blend of east and west, the old and the new-ish, the received wisdom and the one that is being constructed daily. This could be called a form of transmigration or perhaps I am living up to the potential that I have unconsciously embraced in my psyche.

Whatever the argument or back-story: I am tired of being the object of reductionism. The vibrant, intelligent and insightful woman inside me is reduced to the outward appearances of brown skin and country of origin. This happens all the time even after almost a half century in this land... If they don't ask directly – where are you from? they make oblique statements like 'I was in your country twenty years ago and I saw blah....' trotting out stereotypical images and views say of a woman with two baskets piled on her head and a rope around a buffalo. What am I supposed to do or say: 'how clever you are because you have deduced that I am of south Asian origin?

Perhaps they are trying to make some common ground with me but their unwillingness to accept me as a fellow citizen annoys me. In remarks as those cited, I detect some measure of being patted on the head or patronised as I term it. My hackles begin to rise when people do not look straight into my eyes and converse in a normal manner, the way they do when they talk to people like themselves i.e. white people. So many white people when they see me in a group of predominantly white people assume that I am the most ignorant or uneducated of the lot. Their eyes glaze over as they see me in the group and pass over me to ask the nearest white man or woman for directions or explanations, because this 'little brown woman' could not possibly have local or current knowledge let alone understand them and give them a satisfying and erudite answer.

BORN INTO BLOOD AND TEARS

I was born during the monsoon or the rainy season in northern India, which comes between June and early September. The word 'monsoon' derives from an Arabic word 'mawsim' which means the season. It is the season when heavens weep, the land turns green, cool winds blow, mud is everywhere, but the people on the land are happy. Nature's blessings of rain will allow the crops to grow and the cycle of life to continue.

For me, a reference to monsoon means it is the season to talk about myself and the events in the cycle of life which brought me to face my highs and lows, surmount obstacles and get to my destiny. It is now my time to be out there – reflecting and enjoying the harvest in my life.

I was born during the monsoon, a few days before my country of origin, India, gained independence. But this freedom came in the midst of violence and horror. It was accompanied by bloodshed and a hatred of epic proportions. Hindus and Muslims, driven by religious beliefs, fled in opposite directions – Muslims to the west to what is now Pakistan and eastwards to what is now Bangladesh, and Hindus and Sikhs to what is modern India. It was the time of Partition and one of the worst massacres in Indian history, when millions died in the name of religion. The sinister and bloody war of Partition cast its ugly pall on the India which had been tolerant and accepting of all faiths and ethnicities for thousands of years.

I was born under what must have been a grave and sickly moon. Very likely a 'bloody' moon full of anger and hatred and bloodshed, accompanied by an ugly constellation of stars. Mars and Saturn were in their ascendant and at the peak of their battle, when countries reeled under the burden of bloodshed and the virulent rivers of hatred and anger. And that has been the story of my life – experiences of anger and violence, great changes as Saturn is wont to do, losses and gains. It is not a story of peace, steadiness, and harmony.

Kali, the consort of Shiva (one of the gods of the Hindu trinity) ruled supreme at that time – hence it has been called 'Kal Yug' or the age of Kali. Often depicted as a bloodthirsty goddess, she got a river of blood to bathe in, to drink, to dance in and to disperse to the corners of the world. Could this baptism of blood and hatred foreshadow that I would be Kali's disciple? I believe it was more likely a form of inoculation; that my immersion into the rivers of blood, abuse and anger would lead me to become courageous, outspoken and never allow anyone to get the better of me. Perhaps, this has also made me hyper-vigilant but ready for the metamorphosis which would take place when I was ready.

The stories I recount were passed on to me by my grandparents and parents, the horrors they experienced and the bloodshed they witnessed as they sought to 'save' relatives or do their duty as required by their government leaders. The spiritual, emotional and physical violence experienced by the people who witnessed the events cast its influence not only on them but also those that followed. The trauma was so overwhelming that many were unable to come to terms with it and was passed on from the generation of survivors who directly experienced or witnessed the events to future generations via various post-traumatic disorder mechanisms such as parenting practices, behavioural problems, violence, substance use and mental health issues. Such is the nature of inter-generational or trans-generational trauma.

An astrologer who cast my stars during my middle years said I had been born in the eleventh House, the House of Loss! I reacted with horror on hearing this; however, she explained that the 'House of Loss' represents the learning of lessons in this life – bitter, sad, happy, painful - which can strengthen me as I endure the hard knocks and help me to make better or different life-changing decisions. Looking back, my life has been filled with lessons which would make many tremble – changing homelands, traversing continents, undergoing violence and abuse, and overcoming obstacles such as poverty, sexism and racism which at the time seemed taller and more substantial than icebergs and icy mountain peaks.

AN INTERFAITH INDIAN CHILD

When I describe my heritage, some say I am a 'mixed breed' child or an 'interfaith mongrel'. I was born to a couple who would characterise the modern and emerging face of India. Dad was an upper caste Hindu from southern India with a pedigree which went back hundreds of years. My mother was a Christian from northern India, whose own heritage was unique. Her mother was born a Hindu from the trader caste in southern India, but was stolen as a child and converted to Christianity, while her father had Sikh and Hindu antecedents. My maternal grandparents, born at the turn of the twentieth century were educated, middle-class Indians with wonderful social values which they transmitted to their children and grand-children. They were courageous, outspoken and compassionate. They were also social activists in their community and their beliefs were ahead of their time. Their remarkable stories appear at the end of this book so you can read and understand the impact they had on me.

I was the second daughter and the second child. My father named his older children after Hindu gods and mythological characters, all renowned for their feats. He refused to give us ordinary names or those with little history or meaning. I think he was setting out his hopes for us and, in its own way, it mapped out the path we had to follow. I was named after a Hindu goddess renowned for her beauty and virtue, who straddled the line between domesticity and divinity and is an icon for all who deal with impossible husbands or children. The name in itself would serve as an 'omen' – I would need to be both a domestic goddess as well as have the qualities of a saint or goddess to deal with my family.

I had to live up to the destiny that he was setting out for me. Be good, be great, be well-known but do not be forgotten!

When they married, my parents had made a pact of sorts and decided their children would be free to choose their own way of life. This meant in Hindu terms that I had one foot on the ladder to *nirvana* and the other foot on the lowest rung of incarnation. Perhaps I had been an ant or a cockroach or amoebic slime in previous lives. Whatever, but I believe my feet were set too wide apart on the twin ladders to incarnation or *nirvana* and the ladders kept slipping further and further apart. This made living a good life seem daunting and sometimes confusing.

I inherited a thirst for knowledge from both my parents; though, from my father I got a special facility for doing maths in my head. Our home atmosphere fostered in me a huge intellectual curiosity and a love of learning, something which has never left me. From my father, I also received the gifts of independence, clear-sightedness, career-focus, ambition and upward mobility. And perhaps also a deep spirituality which did not derive from religion; he came from an ancient line of priests and scholars who had bridged the divide between temple and academia. Though born into conservative family, he embodied the face of the new India. He joined the military as a young man during World War II when Britain first tried affirmative action i.e. inducting and training Indian men in the ways of the Royal Armed forces and the pomp, splendour and philosophy of colonialism. The magic of the army, its life and the traditions that he learned as a young man, would always stay with him and influence all of us, his children.

I believe the genes were strong due to this cross-fertilisation. From my mother's side of the family, I inherited independence, self-sufficiency, outspokenness, questioning the status quo and a will to never give in particularly when it was a matter of personal values and life beliefs.

I was also fortunate to be the beneficiary of a family philosophy of liberalism and a deep belief in educating its women. Maybe this liberalism and interrogating the status quo to find its reason caused me to question so-called given traditions and beliefs. This led to me being vaccinated early in life against racism and sexism (and attendant discriminatory and stereotypical beliefs) as I struggled to find my place in a world of people of all levels of intelligence, tradition, culture, religion, family backgrounds and ethnicities.

With such parentage, I believe I was part of the vanguard of modern Indian women. I became the third generation of women to be educated and liberated, to go to college (university), the first to have a career and the opportunity to choose my own husband... all these were great feats in their own right. What seems to have also been bred into me along with my mother's milk and dinner at the extended family's dining table was to have community spirit, an attitude of service to those who needed assistance, to be an upstanding citizen and show all the moral and social values befitting my upbringing as the child and grandchild of free-thinking, educated 'Anglophiles'.

Thus I was a child of modern India. While my soul would be filled with eastern wisdom I also grew to love the individualism of the West. In particular, I came to love the rise of independence and equality in the century and country of my birth including the dismantling of the caste system. I trod the path of equality as shown by the prevailing 'isms' of the twentieth century including feminism and egalitarianism as embodied in a democracy. I had the desire to speak my mind and truth instead of kowtowing to colonial or country rulers or family patriarchs. With a myriad of positive qualities and traits bestowed on me by my parents and grand-parents, I found myself drawn to the numbers of women who were finding their own voice, pursuing their own journeys and gaining power they so justly needed after centuries of patriarchy and being told to be mute.

A CHILD OF COMPASSION AND WILDNESS

At the time of my birth, I was an innocent child, full of compassion, unknowing and ignorant of what life would hold. Yet the wild, inner child in me also knew cultivation and grace like the white roses, jasmine and magnolia that proliferated in my grandparents' garden. I was surrounded by tradition but not brought up with traditional thought or patriarchal philosophy. From my earliest years, equality and compassion went hand in hand, like twin sisters. As a child growing up in northern India, I was dismayed by the poverty and lack of equality caused by caste and class differences and economic circumstances that I saw around me. I had the good fortune to be brought up by men and women who, while seeking their own national freedom, would value the freedom and opportunities it would bring to others.

I remember my 'behaviour' would often cause my mother to quote a well-known nursery rhyme about a little girl who had a little curl right in the middle of her forehead, who could swing from being very good to being horrid. The nursery rhyme did not say why but I suspect the pendulum swings when personal boundaries or deep beliefs are threatened or crossed to bring about the change in demeanour.

That nursery rhyme is commonly quoted to young girls to make them 'behave' and fall in line with parental and societal expectations.

It was meant to tame my 'wild' and outspoken nature. In outward appearance, I did not have a curl. I had long straight hair and often walked around with a scowl on my face. My sister once told me I had a 'rhino' nose because it had an upward bump at the end. I spent hours examining it in the mirror. I had full lips, particularly when I had spent hours chewing on them anxiously, making my older sister wonder if I had African ancestry. I had light brown skin, the lightest colour in the family, which was a saving grace in India. But my skin colour was certainly not light enough when I arrived in a white Anglo society.

While I was soft-hearted and kind, I would become ferocious when confronted by inequality and injustice, sometimes overcome by sadness yet seeking joy. I was a child drawn to the spiritual in nature, religion, tradition and universal kindness and peace. I did not feel drawn to one religion or the other but I would be influenced by my grandparents' Christianity, a kind of Anglicanism-cum- Methodism-cum-Protestantism, then my mother's search for 'true' Christianity which became more fundamentalist and literalist in nature as I grew older. From my father, I absorbed the vast embrace of Hinduism and its temples, sages and philosophers who surrounded me.

I was an unruly child but driven by the values that appealed to my spirit and psyche. I showed both bravado and *bonhomie*, was playful but loved learning and came to academic excellence early in life. I knew very early in life that I had a keen mind and was willing to hone it to a razor sharp skill to outwit any one. I valued intelligence as a child more than good looks or was it because I had an older and younger sister who were considered classically beautiful that I opted for cleverness. I don't know. I do know that I still value intelligence and quick wit over beauty for the advantages it brings.

I grew up both wild at heart and also caring and loving in a special way. I projected care and love for those I felt were not as economically blessed. I think this was due to my grandparents' influence, in particular, or it could be some combination of genetic 'softness' within me as well as my upbringing. In another time I would have been named Mercy or Charity because these qualities drove me.

I was a 'free child', often a 'wild child', a child of aspiration and a child who would eventually come into her own. I thought of myself as a female Robin Hood, a lover of justice, stealing from the rich (in this case my parents and grandparents) to give to the poor around me. Years later, I would read the life of a woman, born into a poor agricultural labouring family located no more than fifty miles from where I lived as a child, who went on to lead a gang of bandits. She was raped and mistreated by upper-class men but would live to wreak dreadful vengeance on the ones who mistreated her. I would see the parallel of our lives that wealth or poverty is no determinant of fate or living a comfortable life. I would realise that we were infected and responded to the same *zeitgeist* – women trying to survive and helping their community and downtrodden women standing up for themselves and fighting back.

Having a soft heart meant that I was easily manipulated and this is a reaction I have to reflect on to this day. I thought nothing of stealing from my parents' and grandparents' wallets to help poor people, taking the dinner off their plates and once, the cardigan off my mother's back. One day I discovered a poor labourer's son shivering with cold. His sister told me they were trying to knit him a warm vest but they had no wool. Off I went to my mother's knitting basket to steal yards of wool from various skeins and hand them over. Months later my mother remarked that the poor boy on the street had a woollen vest similar to those she was knitting for my brother and myself. I grimaced and tried to change the subject but was caught out when she ran short of wool and had to resort to another dye lot. She put two and two together and knew I had been up to my 'Robin Hood' pranks.

My earliest emotional memories and feelings are of joy, courage, justice, compassion. These are combined with a boundless energy which seems to flow through the earliest parts of my life. And in between there are rivers of sorrow and despair which I could not fathom as a child. I would cry when I saw a child without a meal or a beggar woman without a shawl or blood on the ground as a headless chicken ran around. Those feelings are still strong in me today as a mature woman.

I could speak three languages before I was three and would learn to read the Bible in all three languages. I also learned to swear by the time I was three or four years old, perhaps from the household staff or Dad and uncles. I would mutter swear words and imprecations as I walked around the garden or played with my siblings. For this I would be reported by the household attendants to my mother or grandfather. My dearly loved maternal grandfather would either laugh at my audacity or defend me when he found me being punished by my mother. This would lead me into more arguments with my mother accompanied by a whack across my arm or leg with one of my mother's rubber slippers. But nothing stopped me. I was deeply afraid of my mother, her fierce temper and her handy cane or rubber slippers, her weapons of choice. Years later I found out that this use of footwear to beat children was not unique to my mother but common in India and south Asian countries. A friend recently told me that her mother, like mine, often told her children that she slept with one eye and one ear open in order to control her children. When the children planned revolt or what was considered remotely anti-family or anti-traditional, her mother would yell from the other side of the room, 'Do you want to meet my slipper?'

My rebellious behaviour and challenging of authority was not quelled; it led to more curses and plotting further mischief as I wandered in the garden. Life seemed to be a succession of being 'tattled' on and retaliating with curses. However, this 'foul-mouthed' child was also getting a balanced upbringing as I my social conscience was being activated.

However, the 'wildness' or 'outspokenness' would be driven out of me by marriage and fundamental religion during my early adult years. It would take me to get to middle age and older to reclaim myself and get my voice back. In my later years, this love of equity or a hatred of inequality would propel me to become a social activist in the spheres of women's rights, careers and pay equity, freedom from domestic violence, and the need for equal voices and opportunities for women of colour.

LIVING A 'GRAND' LIFE

I loved my maternal grandfather with a fierce devotion and in turn he loved me and taught me what he knew –values and social mores, history, geography, astronomy, travel, and most of all social justice. I was also deeply in awe of my wise grandmother, an epitome of social values such as forgiveness, generosity, concern for others, patience and kindness. Above all, her moral courage knew no limit – she spoke and lived her inner truths at all times. Both lived by Christian principles instilled in them - Do all the good you can. Do not live for yourself. They instilled the same living principle in their children and grandchildren. (The remarkable life stories of my grandparents and parents whose values and principles would leave indelible marks on my psyche and soul appear towards the end of this book).

I also learnt social mores and standards of how to behave in polite society and to be upstanding in the community. My grandparents exemplified the bedrock social values of compassion, justice and caring. My moral compass was set early in life by observing their examples of courage and honesty, leavened by large measures of compassion and modesty. They were considered financially well-to-do in their community but would use what they had to help the needy and downtrodden. I emulated them in every way including stealing money from my parents and grandparents, giving away food and household articles and speaking for the ones who did not have the courage or the social status as the occasion arose.

I loved the natural universe which was inherited from and fostered by my grandfather. I was born and lived a large part of my first fifteen years in my grandparents' family home – which was fondly referred to as the 'nest of the nightingale'. My grandfather felt it represented a place where he heard the happy voices of his children and grandchildren. He was very proud of his garden which he had designed himself and for which he won many city awards. (He did have a full-time gardener to do the work but its beauty and creativity inspired him.) I thought of it as a paradise, likening it in my mind to the Garden of Eden, as I ran around the huge and beautiful garden consisting of lily and lotus ponds, exotic and common trees, plants and flowers, both perennials and annuals. One of my morning frolics was to gather flowers from bushes and trees and make garlands to drape across doorways, dressing table drawers and the backs of chairs. This is what drove my grandparents' family and home life – love of their children and grandchildren, creating an oasis of peace and beauty for all to enjoy and serving the community they lived in.

Mealtimes were social and learning occasions. We had a butler and a cook along with two or three other household attendants. The family sat around a dining table – adults and children - eating a balanced and varied cuisine and talking about life and daily activities. I remember lunches being oriented towards Indian food with dinner focusing on 'English' or western food. Conversations around the dining table were lively and we were encouraged to participate - the adults talked about current affairs, what they had read or experienced, stories of yesteryear and answering children's questions. Often they reflected on how things had turned out and steered the conversation towards work or activity which focused on social justice and acts of compassion. I thought everyone had this sort of life. However, as I grew up I realised that either people ate in silence or in front of a blaring television; that many an argument erupted over a dinner table when dishes could be thrown and people punched into the bargain.

Often times, people dropped in to visit and were always welcomed with cool drinks such as homemade lemonade or home-made ice-cream and watermelon slices in summer to cups of tea and cake in winter. It seems idyllic and that is exactly how I remember it. If it was late, the guests would be invited to stay for dinner and the meal would be extended in ways that did not make them feel they were intruding.

The best times were early in the morning in the garden and then late in the evening – listening to stories from my grandparents and parents. The talk would range freely – these were not bedtime stories as such but memories of the past, happenings at family occasions and tales of travel to distant lands where the 'northern lights' were seen or days expanded to late at night. Often times, Grandpa would look up at the stars and point out various constellations and the talk would turn to the past and when we could see a star or comets in the future. They are the stuff of dreams because what we would do soon or far into the future would be spoken of and discussed.

On one such occasion, my grandmother described to us how she had seen Halley's comet in the skies in southern India (1910) where she had lived as a little girl. I could not visualise it so she got me to fetch a pencil and a pad of paper and drew it for me with her arthritic fingers. She was teary-eyed when she finished drawing probably because of the memories that haunted her from that time of her life. She told me she remembered the stories about Halley's comet that circulated among her parents and the community; it was rumoured to bring large scale or global upheavals and it certainly did that in her life. (Read her story towards the end of this book. She went to a English-speaking school with her two sisters for an education, where they were whisked away overnight from their family to be brought up in another place and religion. Reason: they liked the Christian stories and experience. Their experience was part of the colonial philosophy of 'assimilation' which has taken place in many countries like Australia, India and Canada among others. It was considered that children so removed from their families and placed in foster homes or institutions would gradually lose their identity in the wider community and become civilised members of society.)

Her narrative inspired me to look up to the skies and wonder when I would see such a great sight. I was captivated by the shooting stars and constellations amid the galaxies in the night skies, which was heightened by Grandpa's comments about their names and how long they took to orbit earth and other planets and suns. It would be many years till I saw Halley's comet for myself (1986) in the night skies above Melbourne but in the meantime I kept wishing on stars and other astronomical phenomena that were visible to me. Grandma's story made me wonder how a comet in the heavens could have an effect on people on earth but I derived inspiration from it. The picture captured my imagination and I pondered what it would be like to 'hitch my wagon to a star'. To this day, I love looking at stars, eclipses, fleeting comets and astronomical sights because I think of the distances in time and light years and wonder how the lives of earthlings change by the time they see the light of a distant star.

I started reading at three years of age and progressed quickly. I loved comics with heroes like the Phantom and all kinds of adventure books. The heroes of my youth were Robin Hood and his generosity to the poor; the adventures of children as they played detective, their spirit of curiosity and search for truth; and magical figures, who lived in distant African jungles heightened in me a love of the outdoors and a willingness to confront those who terrorised my friends and siblings.

Besides reading western literature, our mother and grandmother loved reading us Bible stories. Later my mother added fairy tales, and at another later stage took to reading us tales of horror (about man-eating tigers) as well as ghost-stories. Bible stories aside, we were also exposed to tales of Hindu gods and goddesses. Due to the diverse faiths of my parents, we were sent to churches of various denominations and Hindu temples. We went to Sunday school and sometimes my siblings and I were sent to pray and chant with little-known religious groups and at other times to Sikh temples for lunch and singing devotional songs.

At age seven, I was introduced to great literature – mostly Western – though I was also encouraged to read translations of Persian, Muslim and Hindu literature. I felt sadness and confusion with *Tess of the D'Urbervilles;* marvelled at the intricacies and traditions of English society after reading *Pride and Prejudice;* wondered about a better way of life after *Utopia*; pondered about sex, adventures and the terrifying consequences after reading *1001 Arabian Nights* (at age ten); saw madness and badness with *Jane Eyre*; wondered if I had an ugly face but a beautiful body as in *Precious Bane*; felt fear and horror after reading umpteen supernatural stories; and felt the twinges of romance for a whole four years between thirteen and seventeen when I read a number of popular romances, to toss them aside and never take them up again after I left my teenage years behind. I read the *Bhagavad Gita,* the wonderful synthesis of Hindu ideas about faith, devotion and the path to salvation; the stories by Premchand a late nineteenth century writer in Hindi-Urdu literature and the poems of Kabir and Mirabai, venerable Indian saints from the middle ages. Then in middle age I came to psychology, philosophy and self-development along with women's studies particularly intersectional feminism.

A much read dictionary, a handbook of metaphors, synonyms and antonyms, a thesaurus, an abridged encyclopaedia and several sets of bound comics sat on built-in shelves next to the toilet seat in one of the bathrooms. If one of us (children) used a 'big' word at dinner time, my mother would accuse us of sitting too long on the toilet seat. She in her turn kept a detailed Railway timetable, next to our bound comic books and dictionary, and would spend her time in the toilet planning her 'escape' to some remote part of the country. I always wondered why. I know Dad was often away on army manoeuvres and would come home once or twice a year for a few weeks. My mother spent the rest of the time pining for him and waiting for his letters which always started with 'Dearest'. The railway timetables looked extremely complicated, because the railway gauges changed from State to State and trains had to be changed at various junctions and took days to get anywhere. But these fitted in with her logical mind, her planning abilities and were her 'escape routes' to the romantic idylls she craved so she pored over them daily.

My love of reading was shared by my siblings. By the time we were in our teens, we competed to read books. We raced through our grandparents' library, through school libraries and books bought by our parents ranging from religious and spiritual books to horror, crime, espionage and any other genre that was around. In a town where we lived when I was fifteen, Dad came home one day to tell us that the Club he belonged to and where he met his army mates and sometimes played cards, had a huge lending library. We raced to join this library and discovered that we could get ten books out at a time. After that, my siblings and I raced to get through a book out of the pile of ten so that we could start on the next one and not wait our turn while the others finished reading their book. This led me to naturally learn speed-reading, for which I am grateful to this day. Over the years as I have moved homes, one of my most urgent errands in my first few days in a new home or suburb is to find the local library and join it as soon as I can. I also buy books but at the rate I read I would need thousands of dollars a year and several spare rooms to store my books because I could not bear to throw them away.

Besides wanting to read and learn art and craft, I kept honing my intelligence and acumen. I can remember being amazed that I could change conversations easily (I called this ability 'flying a kite') by drawing attention to, say, a plane flying overhead, knowing that the conversation would inevitably turn to Grandpa's last travel adventure or Dad's moves or our own future travels to places unknown. Perhaps it was a form of manipulation and steering conversation to areas I wanted to explore. I don't know where that ability came from – perhaps from listening to my father or grandfather who would analyse people's conversations to the *nth* degree to work out their motives and modus operandi.

This perceived cleverness put me into the frontline for taking care of household matters when our parents were absent or unavailable. I remember an occasion when my grandmother died. I was nine years old and we were living in a town two hundred and fifty kilometres or 130 miles away. Our parents received a telegram on a Sunday morning with the news. My mother collapsed in tears and while Dad consoled her, I asked my Dad's army batman to get my mother's suitcase down and started putting clothes and toiletries into it. Then I went to the cook and asked him to make some sandwiches for Mum's lunch and ordered a taxi to take her to the Railway station at 11:30 am. I had remembered that the only train to our grandparents' home town left around noon and if she wasn't on it, she would be delayed by another day. At 11am, Dad came racing to make the same arrangements and was amazed that I had anticipated and done what was required. He called it 'leadership' and foresight. After that, my mother would ask me to look after household matters when she was away from home – whether it was managing grocery replenishments or paying bills or arranging maintenance and repairs.

Don't think I was a bookish nerd. Far from it. I was an energetic, mischievous and fun-loving . I loved to climb trees, play cricket and marbles with my brother; participating in games like 'I spy' and 'statues' with siblings and friends; and playing on my own with my dolls. I had twelve dolls whose names all began with Rose – Rosemary, Rosalie, Rose-Anne, Rosie, Rosalind ... This passion for dolls continued till I was ten years old when I found that one of my doll's faces had been chewed up by a rat in a garden storage room. Dad found me weeping copiously, and consoled me by saying that he would soon bring me a little, live dolly; this was my young sister who was born a few months later, who would become my closest sibling.

I loved to nurse injured animals and people. Dad often teased me and call me 'Nursey'. By the time I was eight or so, he had discovered the diplomatic part of me. The fighting part of me was minor; the peacemaking part was major. He would convince my mother to 'stage' a fight with him in order to watch me run from parent to parent trying to help them make up.

I was the second-born of five children; the first three of us were born very close together. My parents seemed to have wanted two boys and one girl. But like my mother's side of the family, they got two girls and a boy in the first three or four years of married life. The first was a girl and was much loved – and doted on. When I was born eighteen months later, it was ho-hum - not another girl. The very night I was born, my sister wandered in, looked at me lying next to my mother and with tears in her eyes said 'baba' and insisted on getting into bed with my mother. I was placed in a cot next to my mother's bed. And this was my experience for the rest of my growing up years. My older sister always wanted to be in first place – next to Mum and Dad – while I was assigned to be with a Nanny or an Aunt. And when my brother arrived eighteen months later, my mother's life was complete.

This I believe contributed to our sibling jealousies. Families and siblings deny or distort their realities or is this a reality only in each sibling's mind of who got what, when and in what quantity. We remain aware of each other's faults and weaknesses to the utmost degree and continue the judgement and competition forever in our lives both consciously or unconsciously. Someone once said that the family dynamic can be internally fractured yet seem externally united... a bit like a crazed porcelain mug – good enough for tea but it can be shattered if too much pressure is applied.

The jealousies set up in infancy remained for a long time. Our fights, or rather my accusations, were always about who got what, when and where. Who had to stand second or third in line which was inevitably me. However, late in her life, my mother acknowledged that I had not carried over my jealousy or judgement into adult life. The small contentions of childhood had been left behind; when I was in my twenties with a baby I came to understand my mother's love, agonies and frustrations over each child. My mother would confide in me in her later years that she felt comfortable in her relationship with me and the compassion and non-judgemental behaviour I displayed to her.

According to text-books on birth order in the family and the formation of personalities, whenever a second-born child enters the family, his or her life-style is determined by the perception of his or her older siblings. It seems that middle children can be real paradoxes – some can be quiet and shy and others sociable, friendly and outgoing; some aggressive looking to get into fights and others will do anything to avoid conflict. They feel the squeeze from both above and below them in the family. In therapy, the counsellor has to learn to look at the whole family to get a sense of why and how the middle child became the way she is.

When I was ten years old, my younger sister was born. I saw her and fell in love with her instantly. This deep connection has continued to this day and remains a source of great friendship and enjoyment to me. There seems to be a pattern in our family that siblings eight and ten years apart have a stronger bond than those who are close to them in age. A younger brother was born seven years later, who is closest to the sister just before him in birth order. My parents had two families of children, three older ones and two younger ones and when we compare notes, it seems we almost lived different lives.

The dynamic of being the middle sibling in the older lot of three children, and later a sibling among five children born over a period of eighteen years, kept changing. I always felt I had to fight more and that it was harder for me to get something from my parents. Perhaps the scoreboard always exists in our brain. And sometimes it morphs in strange ways - to getting ahead of others in one's academic, social and professional life.

With hindsight, I am glad it was this way. It made me determined to work on the skills and innate strengths that I possessed and the activities that I was drawn to. It led me to study and work to become super-intelligent, super-educated, super-determined and super-successful, to be the first to do or achieve something. Within this construct, I was determined never to be invisible. There was so much riding on me getting ahead instead of being the middle, forgotten child.

EDUCATION AND THE ROAD TO EMPOWERMENT

I had a comfortable or perhaps luxurious life growing up, so I felt no need or desire to be a super woman or a feminist. I had everything I needed and wanted – a mansion to live in with eight or ten household attendants, holidays, chauffeur-driven cars, private schools, entry to university/college. One of my mother's detractors remarked: 'Her children are so spoilt that a nanny wakes them in the morning, leads them to the bathroom and even puts toothpaste on their toothbrushes!' That's the way we were and we did not think this particularly unusual. We were brought up in a material, moral and spiritually rich environment by parents and grandparents who wanted educated children – boys and girls - who would marry well, make charming and educated society hostesses, do good in the community, have two or three children and never have to raise a finger to work.

I went to school at the age of three but my kindergarten teacher noted on my report card that I was very 'nervous'. I needed to go to the toilet every half hour. I would leave my class and go to my older sister's class, get her teacher to excuse her, and hold her hand so she could accompany me to the toilet. Later, I solved the mystery of my nervousness! I realised that during my first couple of years at school we were in the care of our grandparents while my parents lived in an army cantonment town which had no 'appropriate' schools. I was also a sleepwalker and had to be constantly rescued by a nanny or grandparent; sometimes I talked as I walked around the house at night and my night travels were apparently in search of my parents. It was only when our parents took us with them to their next army posting that my nervous behaviour by day and somnambulism by night stopped. My recent studies in psychology and neurobiology have helped me to understand the effects of childhood trauma – separation from parents being a prime factor - which has biological and psychosocial effects in children. Exposure to childhood trauma can activate the body's biological stress response systems with behavioural and emotional effects similar to PTSD (post-traumatic stress disorder). The child's biological stress response is felt in the body's different, interacting systems, which work together to direct the body's attention toward protecting the individual against environmental life threats often toward a fight/flight/freeze/submit reaction.

I had begun by doing well at school – in fact too well – so that by age seven I had skipped a class and landed in the same class as my older sister. I don't know her reaction but she certainly could not have liked it. My classmates were now more advanced emotionally, socially and developmentally than I. The trauma of moving home, moving classes, being with older children led to an educational and emotional stagnation and I spent the next few years in a cluster of students around the middle of the class, hating Algebra and Geometry, but loving History and English.

I came into my own around age twelve or thirteen when I experienced a light bulb moment. I began to work assiduously and get good grades. I discovered I had a quick, natural intelligence, loved all kinds of arts, wanted to learn all about the world and that I was very proficient at the written word. I have wondered what happened to get me to lift my game, so to speak. Perhaps being in the same school living in the same town as our grandparents for three or four years in a row instead of moving every year or two when Dad's army life led us to his next posting. It could also be my grandfather's unfailing love and support and steering me towards great literature and art. This led me to excel in English literature and composition. One day in my second last year of high school, I wrote an essay which earned the top mark in the class. When the English teacher announced that I had the highest mark in the class, the girl who normally got the top marks in the class burst into tears. This in turn drew the attention of my English teacher. Instead of complimenting and encouraging me, she cut me down with scathing words, telling me not to think too much of myself because I had received the top mark for my essay. I was both bewildered and aggrieved. But a light-bulb went on in my brain - I discovered I could actually be good at something i.e. writing. This fed into my passion for reading great literature including encyclopaedias and novels of all sorts from an early age. I had absorbed the magic of words and how a person could craft a letter, article or speech which could affect many. After that my self-belief grew and dogged persistence and a desire to excel took over. This culminated with getting my High school graduation certificate (GCE 'O' level) at age fifteen, with a first class and coming third among the private schools' students in the State.

This was one of the rare occasions that my mother showed that she was proud of me and my intelligence. Usually when I showed cleverness and quick wit, she would often put me down by quoting an Indian saying, 'The clever crow eats shit' which meant academic knowledge and verbal cleverness do not equal wisdom. Strangely for an educated woman, she did not like my reliance on academic knowledge and wanted me to be wise and sober, following her advice and counsel just as my siblings did. She did not like independent thought, perhaps understanding at a deep level that this may lead me to unknown and divergent paths. Hers were strange words for a teenager, who was finding her way in life and developing her own thinking and interests. As a well-know psychologist explains in his theory on the 'conditions of worth' - sometimes the words and expectations of others set up decisions which can lead us to success. Often these conditions of worth arise or come from other people's dreams, not our own, and may not align with our natural talents and abilities. They may lead to a life of unhappiness and a lack of fulfilment, which I experienced as a young woman living up to my mother's dreams. Eventually though when I found myself and aligned my inner compass with my own values and beliefs, I would come into my own.

In my teenage years I discovered a lighter, comic part of myself. I found myself observing people closely so that I could mimic them and thus entertain my family and friends. I found real joy in being a comedienne and making people laugh. I would be asked to imitate people we knew in one of their comic or idiosyncratic moments; having paid close attention to their words, expressions and gestures I would be able to carry it off but I had a deep human understanding which allowed me to be kind and not make them look ridiculous or stupid. To this day, I love comedy particularly stand-up comedy. I love understated, self-deprecating sarcasm and wit and the subtlety of British humour as seen in shows like The Office, Yes Minister, Monty Python, Fawlty Towers and shows of a similar genre. In another life, I intend to be a stand-up comic.

I also found great joy in being a member of the debating team. My sister and I represented our college/ University at many events. For this I thank my mother; she made us learn how to speak eloquently and smoothly, clearly using a few key points and combining this with logic and wit. She started us on this road when we were ten and eleven years old. After we overcame our initial nervousness at having to speak before an audience, we became excellent at both impromptu and prepared speeches. We used our intelligence, knowledge of language and speaking skills to be among the winners at debating contests. This skill has stood me in good stead over the years and I find it easy to speak both extemporaneously or after a short rehearsal. I am glad to say that I have rarely felt the overwhelming fear cited by some who have said 'I would rather die than talk in public'.

My high school graduation result meant I could get into medical school, but I was repulsed by the idea of spending six or seven years of my life cutting up corpses and swotting dense text. Dad was keen on my entering medical school and I wish I had listened to him. Perhaps I would have gone on to specialise in Psychiatry as I now understand how my tastes and life directions have developed. In recent years, I have undertaken Psychotherapy study at tertiary and masters level, and use it for my people, culture and coaching work. But I was wilful and resisted his well-meaning efforts to steer me into medicine; instead I decided to do a double major in English Literature and Political Science, entering University in the same year as my older sister. (Could this also be related to my inner belief that I would marry well and have no need of a career?) English Literature may seem a little curious but it fed into and fuelled my love of language, reading and research, particularly the classics. I remain an avid reader to this day – reading at least two or three books a week besides devouring several magazines, e-magazines and other sources of information.

Besides English Literature and Political Science, I also took a minor in Sociology at college. Somewhere along the way, the unconscious wheels in my brain were turning to give me a grounding in issues and ideas which would inspire and interest me for the rest of my life – people, their history, their community, their traditions and customs, their political beliefs, their ways of ruling and administration and the society they create.

Once again I fared well academically, coming in the top ten students in the university (to which our college was affiliated) for that year. I obtained a first class Bachelor of Arts degree, finishing by the time I was eighteen. Academia seemed to have come easily to me and also to my siblings. My older sister and I went through university together and were considered to be all-round stars – intelligent, accomplished, and well-connected, besides being good looking and well-dressed. However, while learning seemed to have come easily to us, we were later to discover as we entered the changing world of the second half of the twentieth century that English literature and Political Science were not going to help us in a career or to earn a living.

THE SLUMBERING FEMINIST – MARRIAGE OR INDEPENDENCE

What did I think I would do with the fine education I had received? I thought I would marry and be a society lady, although this was really at odds with the religion my mother had adopted. And it was her religion which dominated us as teenagers and young adults. Wanting to please my mother really led me down a path which would bring me heartache and sorrow.

I don't really think I knew what I wanted but the general idea was to hold a job for a short while, shortly afterwards get married and then sail through the rest of my life! I know this was the prevailing ethos for women in most places around the world in the middle of the twentieth century and is still alive many decades after. But some of us in the latter half of the twentieth century challenged it and this has affected our daughters. Their lives and expectations have changed because we challenged this 'given' tradition.

After graduating I decided to flex my wings. I wanted to be independent of my parents so I got a job doing secretarial work in another city far from where they lived. In this new city, I had to live very modestly compared to my parents' resplendent lifestyle with their six-bedroom mansion, five or six household staff, leading and entertaining the officer and community elite. They were far removed from the ordinariness that I then began to experience as an independent working woman.

Still thinking of the future, I seem to have had the expectations of my family and my social class in the back of my mind. Like my grandmother, mother and aunt, I expected to be married to some high-flying male, likely a civil or military service officer, oversee a household consisting of a husband, two or three children and a few household staff, and spend my time between social activities and some sort of volunteer community work.

What a fallacy and trap that would prove to be. India like the rest of the world was changing. More critical was my mother's devotion to a fundamentalist religion which ensured that I would not find a man who could keep me in wealth and stay-at-home luxury. Why? Because my mother insisted that we, her children, marry in her religion. The folk in her church were of a different social class, not very well-educated and predominantly from working class, lower-paid occupations. This would prevent me from finding a mate who was my equal in social class, wealth, education and upbringing as the people who flocked to ultra-right, fundamental Christianity espoused by my mother did not share either my intellectual ethos or lifestyle.

My sisters and brother like me accepted the inevitable and found a mate in the church. This would change me from an incipient, forthright, upper-class Indian woman to one who was dominated and humiliated by a man who consciously and unconsciously resented my upbringing and used all his efforts and behaviours to humiliate and subjugate me.

A DISASTROUS FIRST MARRIAGE

My blind-spot which was to be my undoing! I believed I was a clever young woman because I could talk fluently on a variety of subjects, hold intense conversations on political and social issues, do good work in the community and be invited to the most exclusive events in town. However, my academic knowledge and cleverness, blinded me to understanding that I was not smart in the ways of the world. (Thanks, mother, for predicting that the 'clever crow eats shit'.) I was also easily manipulated. This made me prime material for being lassoed by the man I would eventually marry. (As I began to understand his psychology and emotional condition, I realised that there were large elements of narcissism and sociopathy within him.)

Six months after graduating I met a man who belonged to the same religion as my mother. He was sharp-witted and a smooth talker, and he wanted to make his way in the world socially and materially. He was motivated to marry me, as I later discovered, because he saw a young nineteen-year-old woman ripe for the plucking with well-to-do parents of high social standing! After a few months of a postal romance along with my eagerness to live the life my parents had, I agreed to marry him. My father was not very happy with my decision or choice but my mother persuaded him to let me marry and so I did not encounter many obstacles.

I think I saw in myself the proverbial Snow White romance unfolding. I felt I was marrying for love, insisting to my parents that I knew what I was doing and all would be well. Wrong, wrong, wrong. I was naive and infatuated. I now realise that I was not in love, nor did I feel the earth-shattering feelings of love. Perhaps I was in a 'trance' – I believed I needed to get married and start on the next step of my journey. Romance and Married Love 101 was my new agenda. I did not stop to think that I could be marrying the wrong man. My parents provided a lavish wedding and everything required to set up a house and home.

My husband had been born into another race and religion though his mother had converted to Christianity. He carried a deep superiority complex of having 'white' skin that came from what he believed was his racial superiority. Within weeks of our marriage I began to understand how racist, sexist and violent he was. He hated my background and upbringing – a 'hidden' envy - as he had been brought up in a so-called poor country and lived with his parents and siblings in very humble circumstances. I have often wondered why he married me. His hidden racism accompanied by sexism would continue throughout our married life and would knock the breath out of me – both physically and mentally. It also took me many years to realise that he was also had a paranoid personality disorder which made him suspicious and indulge in various malevolent behaviours. In hindsight, I see his cruelty clearly – not just in the intimate partner violence that I experienced, which was conflated with his misogyny, but in his racism and often downright sadism. More on this later.

At the time of my marriage I was ignorant of the facts of life and had never made love to anyone. And he may have been naive too. Whatever it was, he pretended to be know everything. I think he had talked to experienced, prurient men and read books of all sorts on sexual behaviour. Looking back, my honeymoon night was a comedy of errors. We went to a honeymoon hotel in the same city as our wedding. I had a shower and came back dressed in my virginal white see-through white nightgown to discover a large bottle of disinfectant and a huge roll of cottonwool on the bedside table.

'What is that for,' I asked? 'Are you going to perform an operation?' He replied 'It is going to be bloody and painful.' I crossed my legs and crept into bed, refusing to let him touch me. It took three days before I could be persuaded to 'lose my virginity'. It was not the romantic, loving experience I had anticipated or wanted. I was positioned on my back, told to keep my legs apart and not to wriggle or do anything which could ruin his concentration. I felt like a convenient sex-doll or something worse.

And that was to be the story for the next seven years. This was the interaction every night and often times after much verbal abuse and sometimes physical abuse and mental torment during the day. Hardly the loving exchange that I had hoped for – having lived in kind and caring households.

I had committed the dreadful mistake of marrying the wrong man. And I could not break free for two reasons: my heritage – women don't leave their husbands because society does not allow it and they become outcasts; the other reason being the religious beliefs inculcated by my fundamentalist religion that women were to be submissive to their husbands and always remain by their side.

Slowly or perhaps quickly, I fell into 'hell'. A hell not of my making but one which I was too fragile, overwhelmed and depressed to overcome. I entered a stage of my life that I would like to forget. I became a 'slave', a domestic servant, a woman who underwent sex without love, a woman without a voice.

I believe it was the experience of violence and abuse - physical, emotional and philosophical, which made me lose my way and my voice till I was over thirty. In fact, the threat of abuse was ever present. I shudder to think about the abuse I suffered – choked with a rag stuffed down my throat, stabbed in the leg with a sharp pen causing a piece of flesh to fly out and land on the floor, black eyes, blows to the chest and upper arms which could be covered by clothing and being pushed (unsuccessfully by the grace of God) from the back of a motor-cycle after an incident where I had made an innocent remark putting myself down (i.e. being dreadful at packing) which had invoked violent abuse from him for daring to criticise him even indirectly. I trod on egg-shells daily; I could not express an opinion because it would earn me physical blows and slaps and a torrent of abuse ranging from four-letter words to being torn apart emotionally and verbally so that I felt like a worm wanting to crawl away and hide.

The social virtues of justice, equality, compassion and kindness which were ingrained in me as a young child were trampled on daily by my husband and the fundamentalist church we both belonged to. I worked as a slave at home and a six-day slave in an administrative job in the city. I was also totally controlled by my husband, who kept me on a short economic leash and monitored the people who were my friends. My diaries and letters were monitored; any friends I made were criticised and abused in private so that I became afraid to have any friends socially or at work for fear of hearing how bad they were and that I was not to associate with them. I handed my pay-check over every week and received a tiny amount of pocket-money, sufficient to buy a coffee and perhaps a handkerchief. I would also hand over cash bonuses received at work and if I was very good I would be rewarded with a kitchen implement or a dress. I remember teaching myself to sew because the maximum I ever received for a dress was ten dollars or its equivalent! A woman I worked with during the first few years of marriage was to introduce me to the value of having my own bank account and to put aside part of my earnings (from 25-30%) into a savings account in my own name. For this act of independence, I would receive much abuse but I am glad I persisted. These experiences taught me self-reliance and sageness. I also learnt how to make the best of whatever I had. But I lost my free-spirit, my love of learning, my independence. I learnt to be a quiet and wise soul but not a free one. My spirit was broken by a man who was too selfish to know better. Any idea of romance and married love crumbled within six months of being married. And I have not believed in love and romance since my twenties. In fact, I consider myself cynical about romantic love ever since. I have never wanted to fall in love, rarely if ever been infatuated and perhaps seem cool and dispassionate to some. I am ever mindful of the need to protect myself, my sanity and vulnerability.

I did escape for twelve months to live in Europe to live with my siblings who had moved there. And there I found, for the first time, how exciting and fulfilling an independent, single life could be. I found an administrative job in a sales company but also got a taste of an enjoyable social life – movies, opera, dinners, movies, travel and great friendships - all without fear of violence and abuse.

But that did not last long. I was ordered by my husband and 'master' to go back to him. I took the long way home via ship from Europe to India visiting places in Italy, Spain, South Africa and Kenya on the way back – delaying the moment of reunion! This was the early nineteen seventies and I was to have my first encounters with racism in Capetown and Durban. It was during the years of *apartheid* and gave me a taste of what being an inferior human in society could be like. I was appalled not only with the treatment I received from 'whites' but also by the anger and resentment it brought up in me. I found I could not go into cafes where whites went, was not allowed to sit on benches or go to toilets marked whites only nor sit in buses on seats reserved for whites. The only place where I seemed to be welcome was in department stores because the colour of my money was the same as that used by white people. In another port town on my trip back, I came very close to being assaulted and 'raped' as a result of a venture with a friend to a club fifteen miles away from the city proper where our ship was docked. My friend disappeared with someone but I would not follow her example so I took a taxi back to the ship which I was forced to share with the man who had been harassing me and was determined to follow me back to town. The way back to the city and portside was via lonely roads through a jungle. My escape was both serendipitous and farcical. An argument erupted between the local, 'black' taxi-driver and the 'white' male who had forced himself into the taxi with me regarding the apartheid. I seized on the escape provided by the argument regarding racism and fanned the already fiery flames to save myself. While they yelled at each other abusively, their attention shifted from me and I was left alone - forgotten. As soon as we got within sight of the docks - the entry to which was over-shadowed by an enormous pair of cement tusks, I leapt out of the taxi and ran weaving my way down dark docks and drunken sailors to get to my ship. That was enough to cure me of nightclubs and other adventures for years.

Within a couple of months of returning to India, I was pregnant. It was only then that I recognised that I could not bear to be under the same roof as my husband any more – he had been financially, mentally, emotionally and psychologically abusive to me in the five years I had been married to him. But I was stuck: about to have a baby, under the control of a cruel, racist and sexist man, and back in the confines of a restrictive religious regime. I spent most of my pregnancy alone and depressed, lying in bed, staring at the ceiling, rarely going out to have interaction with people.

My loneliness and need for love and care from parents, family and friends was at an all-time high. But I did not reach out to anyone preferring my solitary, stoic life. I was also prepared to help others

In the middle of my own 'tragedy'. Or perhaps I was trying to take my mind off my own sadness.

A couple of months before my daughter was born, I went to visit a new friend, who had married a man twice her age and fond of the bottle. Like me, she was now expecting her first child. Our paths seemed to be similar and we bonded. On knocking at her door one day, I learnt from her husband that she had gone to the hospital the day before. We raced to the hospital where I took charge of attending to my friend while her husband went to the pub. I ran up and down the clinic looking for staff to attend to her, holding her hand between labour pains. Ten hours later she had a forceps procedure in the early hours of the morning. When I came out to tell her husband he greeted me effusively touching my protruding stomach and blessing me like an old-style prophet! Embarrassed, I ran back to my friend. Later I quizzed her about her choice of clinic where neither the doctors nor the nursing staff were interested in helping her give birth. I discovered that some of her friends had been there for abortions ... no wonder there was no interest in a live birth!

Two months later I went into childbirth and had to have an emergency Caesarean section – perhaps brought on by my inability to give birth naturally. My obstetrician insisted that this was a psychological issue, due perhaps to attending my friend's harrowing birthing experience weeks before. According to him, obstetricians did not like women attending others' birthing experiences if they had not had a child of their own. This psychological 'hang-up' caused by witnessing a difficult childbirth was compounded by the attitude of my husband who abandoned me in the hospital while he took care of his business and career. A girl-friend who lived close by came to support me as I laboured to give birth. Forty hours later, I gave birth to my beautiful daughter who would become the centre of my life. I regretted having prevented my mother from coming to help and support me. She lived in a city a thousand miles away, but I thought I was brave and self-sufficient, able to manage any crisis or pain. Going home, I also discovered the lack of support in caring for my baby. These events combined to put me into deep post-partum depression for a couple of years as I struggled to make sense of my life and care for my beautiful child.

JOURNEY TO AUSTRALIA

Soon after my daughter's birth my husband came home to tell me that we were emigrating to Australia. He had applied to emigrate without consulting me. I went into shock, wondering how I would cope in a strange land where I had no relatives or friends. My post-partum depression deepened; I stayed at home and nursed my baby and cried over her little head. Those were not the days of supportive childcare nurses or mothers' groups; I had no one to turn to and did not think of consulting or confiding in someone, not even my family or the few close friends I had. The walls of depression seemed to close in on me; every day was a living nightmare as I cared for my child. Perhaps, the only reason I stayed alive was the love and responsibility I felt for my baby daughter.

My husband was considered appropriate for emigration to Australia, presumably because of his 'whiteness' or race. I went to the consulate and was asked by a condescending, white bureaucrat who asked me whether I would be able to fit into Australia. I felt shocked because he judged me by the colour of my skin colour and not my talents, social background or tertiary education. My one-month-old baby managed to get her own back at him, letting her flatulence loose during the hour-long interview. Yes, baby, yes... she let this man know how he was viewed by people who may have been brown or black but were far removed from him in terms of values, education or social standing.

Coming to a country on the other side of the world was to be a life-changing lesson for me. I was twenty-five years old when we emigrated and my daughter, whom I loved passionately, was nine months old. I was desperately homesick for my family and the affluent life-style I had left behind. Added to this was the black cloud of post-partum depression. Perhaps the isolation and loneliness of a new country was deeply intertwined with my post-partum depression and the two conditions fed off each other.

Australia was still a 'white' country (though it had dismantled the 'White Australia' Policy a few years before) as the consular official had spelt out to me with his patronising words. Indeed coming to Australia was a shock to my system. I knew no one in the country – I had no friends and no support. I knew my husband was ashamed of my colour and race because he constantly asked me to say that I was of southern European descent not Indian – as if that could fool people about my ethnicity. I think he wanted me to be gone or to stay invisible. All he seemed to want from me was either daily sex or to get rid of me and find a partner with one of the white women he had met. At one stage he even suggested that I could live as his housekeeper while he brought another woman to live in our apartment. Perhaps, that was his version of polygamy without the marriage ceremony or it may have been a precursor to getting rid of me.

MISERY – MY STRUGGLE FOR SANITY AND FREEDOM

My early days in my new country are remarkable to me because I was in abject misery. I sat for hours and cried in a corner on my bedroom floor while my young daughter often toddled over to pat me on the head or cuddle me from time to time. I remember my heart being so full of pain that I would often bang my head on the wall – I wanted to feel the physical pain and not the gut-wrenching, heart-breaking pain in my soul. But there was no one to care for me or for me to talk to.

A kind old doctor helped me to stay sane. He came on weekly house visits which were not required of him. These visits gave me the support and care I needed both physically and mentally. My **triple whammy** was now post-partum depression, homesickness and the experience of daily violence which somatised in my body. I contracted glandular fever which kept me in bed or at home and lasted three months. Every day my husband would 'torture' me with words like 'I am waiting for you to die,' 'this is what I will do at your funeral,' 'that's the woman I will get to come into my bed', or 'I will section you (commit you) into a psychiatric ward and then take my daughter away to another city or country.'

When my husband found out about this dear doctor's visits, which had kept me on this side of sanity, he banned me from seeing him.

He went to the doctor's surgery and told him that he was no longer to visit me at home or have me as a patient. Though I was very ill at this point suffering from deep depression (caused and exacerbated by domestic violence and lack of family support) plus the physical effects of glandular fever, I decided to leave home and start afresh. I knew I was on the verge of losing my daughter permanently because my husband had threatened to take her away to another country. The choices were stark: become a long-time resident of a psychiatric ward never seeing my daughter again OR lose my daughter to a man who would affect her mentally and emotionally, fighting without hope to get her back. I reasoned that a single, unsupported life with my daughter still by my side was better than a life of torture and pain and a short journey to madness or death.

Hearing my husband's fateful words forced me into action. Somewhere, somehow, I found the strength in the depths of my depression and pain to do something. I roused myself from my deep despair as I struggled to figure out what was better – being in a psychiatric ward and losing my daughter or leaving my prison-like home for a difficult and unknown life. I did not realise then but do now that my husband was playing the 'gaslighting' game with me. The only one who would listen and take heed was my dear old doctor. I confided in him with sobs, asking him if I was going mad. He comforted me and told me that I was quite sane. When I asked his opinion about leaving because of my pain and fears of going insane, he counselled me to consider the avenues I contemplated seriously. He said he would stand by me but once I started on a course of action, the steps I took would be irrevocable. There would be no going back.

Once this decision was made, I looked at ways to find accommodation and work. One day, I dried my eyes, yanked my psyche and body together and walked, pushing my daughter in her stroller over five or six kilometres (4 miles) to visit a lay preacher and his wife who had been kind to me. I had met them at the church I had gone to for a few months and they had shown their compassion and invited me to their home for lunch. As I walked under a relentless sun along main roads, I felt numb with pain. Tears would not flow freely. I was paralysed with grief and despair. I felt like a beggar, similar to those I had seen in my childhood in India, who had evoked my compassion. When I finally got to their place, they asked me no questions. They fed me and spoke kindly and caringly while I sobbed my heart out . Perhaps this was my moment of personal *karma* or the good wishes and blessings of those I had helped coming back to me – what goes around, comes around.

They said they could give me room for a couple of weeks and help me find a job if I could not get any government help in the form of a single mother's allowance.

A few days later, I went to the government's social services department to ask for help, but the women behind the counter spoke dismissively to me, telling me to go away and get money from my husband for my needs. These insensitive women could see my distress but they had neither compassion nor advice to give as to how to go about getting food and shelter. I spoke clearly and rationally in English but their hostility and disdain for me was very apparent. I walked out crushed. If I had not been holding my daughter's stroller, I would have collapsed on the street and cried.

Now I wonder if this was an example of structural or overt racism? Was my dark skin a deterrent to getting a compassionate and informative response? Or did I experience a sense of superiority combined with disdain for the little brown woman who stood in front of them, asking for help?

I also went to a police station to ask for help but was laughed at by male police officers who thought it was fun to treat me like an insane 'black' (brown, coloured) woman. One asked me, with a knowing wink, if I needed physical comfort saying that he could provide it.

My agony was compounded of psychological, emotional and physical control and abuse. The financial abuse was ongoing from the day I married him. I did not possess ten dollars in cash and certainly had no access to credit cards or a savings account. (Sorry, I forget: I was a signatory to a cheque account which only ever contained two dollars from start to end.) My husband had made sure to keep me on a very tight budget (a real state of dependency and economic abuse I have since learned). I was never given more than ten or fifteen dollars for groceries for which I had to render an exact account. The change in my purse had to tally with the shop dockets I took home. Even my toilet paper was rationed: from behind the bathroom door, my husband would yell at me that he could tell by the rattle of the toilet paper holder that I was using too much paper! So I got into the habit of stuffing tissues into my bra before going to the toilet.

I got ten dollars a year for buying a dress, which led me by necessity to learn and become proficient at dress-making. Perhaps this also accounts for my love of clothes and I gladly change styles and wardrobes from one year to the next. I wore mended dresses if I tore or burnt one. I once bought a pair of shoes for twenty dollars on lay-by (weekly/ fortnightly terms), clawing the money together by saving fifty cents or a dollar out of the vegetable and fruit money or by saying my daughter wanted a doughnut, hence I was a dollar short of change in my wallet. Possessions I cared for because they represented a connection with dear ones in my past life were rudely torn away or disposed of like my grandmother's engagement sari, the gift of an antique brocade skirt from my Aunt's dance career, and a silver samovar and rug from my beloved grandfather. If he knew

I that something held emotional and sentimental values, he would make sure to get rid of it.

I know why I care so deeply for and empathise with women affected by domestic abuse, sexual harassment, discrimination and poverty, because I had experienced all these circumstances at the same time in a strange land.

I feel a great passion to be active in the Domestic Violence space and find funds and resources for women crushed by violence along with isolation and misery. Because domestic violence includes abuse and intimidation on many levels in order to control and dominate the other person. This causes fear, physical harm and/or psychological harm and leads to isolation and depression.

Domestic violence includes emotional abuse, physical and sexual assault, verbal and psychological abuse, financial abuse and isolation of the person from friends and family all of which I experienced. But I did not understand the full enormity of what I was undergoing. I knew I was experiencing cruelty and sadism at deep levels. And in my depression and vulnerability, I thought it was my 'fate' to have fallen into the hands of a cruel and controlling man.

Domestic violence is not just a violation of women's rights but a violation of human rights.

LEAVING A HOME OF VIOLENCE - FINDING MY FEMINIST SPIRIT

Despite my early experiences in Australia and as I navigated each step of my awful journey, I was maturing psychologically and emotionally and getting stronger. I lived in two worlds – the daily life of control, poverty and isolation and the other life that was in my head and heart. I was separating myself mentally from this daily violence by looking and planning ahead to the life that I knew would come. I planned for the time when my daughter would begin to go to school and I would be able to get a job. This became my simple plan to free myself of the unjust and cruel bonds. I believe I drew on the confidence and independence inculcated in my early years as a child and teenager. I got the courage to start the journey, however minor or major it may have been initially, because of needing to protect my daughter against the insanity and violence of our home environment and also because of the acid of injustice that was corroding my soul.

I am reminded of the work of a psychologist, who outlined his ideas about the various stages of life and said that we grow not just physically but also through the inner conflicts we face as we mature and the relationships we have. Another psychiatrist I read added the notion of our personalities being like 'chairs of identity' with each of the four legs representing trust, autonomy, initiating action and being industrious. The seat of the chair is our main identity; however, in the course of our lives we mature and heal and the chair gets re-shaped.

Sometimes the chair gets wobbly and needs repairing but we are always shaped by the early materials we had or were taught to work with. Perhaps the traits of my childhood - my innate justice, love of independence and self-sufficiency – helped to re-mould me so that I stayed true to my original personality and traits.

Trying to leave a home of violence with my two-year old daughter was to be the first of three or four attempts at independence and running from abuse. A couple of times I confided in church members and elders from my fundamentalist church asking them for help, but invariably someone would betray me because they believed in the sanctity of marriage and the headship of the man. Many a so-called committed-to-the Bible elder would invoke the guilty feelings of the person I had confided in and asked for help. I know my husband and others like him including the church elders wanted women to be slavishly devoted to their husbands and that they should look forward to their reward in the next life. But if they wanted that sort of blind devotion they should have got dogs! I think many church elders were also afraid that rebellion like the one I was experiencing would infect their wives too! And so it did. In the last few years, I have heard of several women married to men of this ilk who left them and went on to live alone because of the lack of personal care and human comfort that they experienced during their married years.

Years later, I was mesmerised when I watched the series 'The Handmaid's Tale' on television, the 'theocratic' culture it displayed and the uncanny resemblance to the behaviours of the men and women I had once associated with. This is a culture that has flourished in some fundamentalist churches, where they argue that they are closely following biblical teachings.

Only once during those painful years did I receive encouragement from a supportive church elder when he asked me to lay out my domestic experiences before the entire body of church elders (ten men). He reasoned that they would see my 'innocence' and would reprimand my husband. They heard but they did not listen with their hearts. They turned me away saying they could not help me to break free or give me 'justice' because as far as they were concerned, we were married in the eyes of God. I believe they were also afraid of my vengeful husband. Additionally, they argued, that if I had forgiven him (through prayer) for the harm done to me via abuse and/or unfaithfulness then the marriage bond could not be broken. Christian teachings were used as a double-edged sword to keep me locked in a loveless and abusive marriage! After every such occasion, when I had appealed to the elders or to a fellow church member, I would be dragged back crying and screaming in real fear for my physical self . This would be accompanied with a barrage of abuse and threats that my daughter would be taken away and I would never see her again. She was all I had. She was the light of my life and I was determined to never let go of her. So I stayed and stayed, planning for the time when we could both be free.

Thus my husband dragged me back two or three times and forced me to live with him. These were years of pain and torture of various kinds – mental, emotional and physical. He spied on me in various ways and made sure that I was isolated and virtually penniless. In hindsight, I realise he 'gaslighted' me constantly and kept control over me. Don't forget, I was not only a prisoner but my unsuspecting daughter was also part of the equation. She loved him but did not understand the full story of what was happening in the home. I feared for her mental and emotional safety as she grew up.

Another two or three years passed. However, my independence and confidence had begun to coalesce into a firm resolve to remove myself from my place of misery starting from the very first point of refusal by church elders, police and government officials. Internally,

I was resolute that I would escape as soon as my daughter was able to go to school and I could get a job and accommodation. I made plans in my head. But I did not show my resolve or plans outwardly. I could not and would not reconcile myself to living a life of misery, torment and lack of freedom. I waited and planned and bided my time - and he guessed it as I found out afterwards. Eventually, I got my freedom but it came at great cost.

People have asked me why I didn't ask my family for help. My pride stopped me. I had insisted on marrying my husband even though they had some misgivings. I also did not want to sadden them. There were no women's refuges at that time. Some people told me to apply for a single mother's government pension/allowance available to single women without spouses in Australia at that time but I rejected this idea. Truthfully, I could not see myself sitting at home and waiting on a single mother's pension cheque and living a life of near poverty. Even if I had done so initially, I think I would have found my feet and a job within a matter of months. Suffice to say, I have never availed myself of a government pension or social service relief.

Still in fear of my husband's wrath combined with my inborn independence and refusal to accept any more 'sass' or advice from white men and women (religious or secular), made me decide to search for employment and to become 'successful' in my own right.

Sometime during these early years in Australia, a friend in the church, I attended gave me a ticket she could not use to go to a concert featuring the singer, Helen Reddy. (This female friend was the only woman who believed me and supported me in my desire for freedom and independence but when my husband discovered her support for me, I was forbidden to see her or talk to her. I did so secretly and I thanked her then and to this day for helping me keep my sanity. She did not live long enough to see me become a fiercely, independent woman.) I did not know of Reddy's music or life values so I was unprepared for the experience. Reddy's music and its lyrics inspired me in my journey to independence and having a worthwhile life. The words of her song 'I am woman' have been with me since the day I heard them and helped me to understand and attain the purpose and passion of my life. The values of justice, strength and equity that I had embraced as a young child finally became meaningful as I began to make my life as an independent and self-respecting woman.

Finally, I became FREE five years after arriving in Australia. When I eventually got out and went into shared accommodation, I felt exuberant and on top of the world. Yes, I was fearful as to how I would support myself and my child. I was almost destitute –a single parent, ten dollars in my wallet and two suitcases of clothes. So much for my parents' expectations - that I would marry well and never need to work. My daughter was only four years old. I managed to get a small administrative job, rented two rooms in a home owned by a kind European woman, who had herself suffered abuse from her own husband. She was also a member of the fundamentalist church that I attended at that time. When the news got around that she would let me live at her place, she received a visit from the church elders warning her to turn me away and not give me shelter. To her great credit, she defied them and said that as long as I lived a good life, looking after my daughter and not taking up alcohol and men, she was going to give me a place to live. Finally, I was safe physically and emotionally from control and abuse. I felt that the heavens were smiling on me!

In time, after a great deal of self-representation in court and some support from a kindly lawyer provided through the Government's legal aid, I was able to get a formal separation and custody of my daughter. I received legal orders for a meagre amount of child maintenance from a man who earned three times what I was earning and lived in the family home which he had managed to keep under his own name. I know it was an extension of the financial and emotional control I had suffered till then. The money for my daughter's maintenance was always predicated on my obedience to my ex-husband's commands and later on my daughter's obedience to his commands, when she went to visit him on week-ends.

A couple of years after I escaped, my ex-husband applied for a 'no fault' divorce even though he continued to vilify me in public and private and in the court, saying that I was the person responsible for the break-up. Initially, I was prevented from going anywhere outside the metropolitan area of the city I lived in and had to ask for written permission to go to another city or travel to another country. I persevered, tackling each obstruction as it arrived. I was finally free to become the woman of independence and spirit that I knew dwelt within me.

In the following years I saw my torture being replaced with my daughter's emotional torture. Watching a series of interactions with her father, I saw her being bullied, punished and emotionally destroyed. But that is her story. My heart would break for her as I watched her come back from weekends with her father – anxious, weepy and distraught. I had escaped but she her punishment continued. This was my own personal tragedy and heartbreak – winning my freedom but at her expense. Other variations of the torture continued over the years and parental visits would stop with the blame being put on me. She would be told at times that she did not love him enough, that her mother was a call-girl, that she could not go with me on holidays. Finally, at age twelve she came to her own decision - that she would see him when she felt she wanted to.

A POSTSCRIPT TO MY UNHAPPY FIRST MARRIAGE

A few years later, I received a letter from my ex-husband which I believe was a means of getting me back. Over eight hand-written pages, he catalogued his wrongs and excesses. I was somewhat puzzled when I received it but it was too late. I was aware that a leopard does not change his spots. I would never go back to him. Later I was to understand that this was typical of the cycle of domestic violence. The perpetrator's actions are repetitive or cyclical in nature and often hinder the victim's ability to leave the abusive relationship. The first stage is the build up of emotional, verbal and financial abuse including nit-picking, put-downs, threats, yelling, isolation, financial control. The second stage is the acute explosion which may have punching, hitting, kicking, humiliation, stalking and verbal abuse. The third stage is the 'honeymoon' or let's make up phase which may include apologies, gifts, agreeing to get help, wanting forgiveness and getting back together peaceably.

He had taken everything from me – furniture, friends, gifts from parents, and jewellery. I later discovered from my daughter that he had given his second wife two rings – both stolen from me when I left the marital home - telling this poor woman that one was an engagement ring he had specially picked for her and the other a wedding present. I suspect he would re-steal them to give to his subsequent wives. The second wife was also thrown aside after a

57

few years when she lost her ability to cook, clean, and minister to his sexual wants as a result of crippling arthritis. I knew and understood that his misogyny was greater than his racism!

I talked to his second wife, shortly after she was pushed aside in favour of a third woman; she wept, saying that initially she had not believed the stories she had heard about me until she suffered the same abusive treatment. She said: 'Now I understand what you went through.' The third woman, who had been a carer for the second wife, was co-opted into an affair; she enjoyed a brief stay in the sun. She too would reap her just rewards; she reached out to me a few years later wanting to know what I had been through. On meeting with me, the third wife said that she would not have believed me before but now understood the abusiveness and torment of this man. Other women have come and gone, but I think none has had the resilience or single-mindedness like myself to survive, grow and thrive.

I did not send him a letter in return. I did not want to – all I had to say had already been said. I had made a new and happy life. If I had, it would have read as follows :

> I would never have behaved the way you did during our marriage ... I would never have done the things you did because they were all so selfish and heartless giving no consideration to my needs or that of our daughter. I would never have argued and fought and reviled you, and made you feel worthless. I would never have hit you or threatened you with violence. I would never have broken you with mental and emotional torture. I would never have made promises unless I intended to keep them ... I guess you never loved me. I would never have left you lying

in bed unable to move, pleading for help; I would not have been mean to you, torturing you with images of bedding other women... I would have been kind to you, supporting you as you made a new life in a new country... I would have made sure you and our daughter felt secure and loved.

THE AWAKENING FEMINIST

A new life and new obstacles

I awoke from my long sleep or a nightmare when I finally walked away from a twisted and tormenting man. And while I fled my persecutor within five years of coming to Australia, I discovered that the structures of racism and sexism, including misogyny and condescending behaviour, stereotypical labelling and emotional abuse in many other areas of life were just beginning.

This was the Australia of the 1970's and the vast majority of Australians had been indoctrinated by the 'White Australia' policy. Very few migrants up to that time had dark skin or non-white ethnicity; the few who did were patronised and patted on the head because they had experienced the great good fortune to come to a wealthy and 'loving' country from their poverty-stricken lives in other countries. I should have realised this as I looked around and saw the discrimination practised against and the misfortune of Indigenous people; I should have known by hearing the words spoken by white people about the Italians, Greeks, Turks, Yugoslavs and Fijians who came to Australia. But my confident inner self thought that this was about others and not about me until I began to take one too many hits of racism and discrimination.

I would be accosted by people who would ask me questions like, 'Are your teeth real?' I wanted to say 'No, they are made of plastic'. Other times I would be asked 'What sort of house did you live in your country?' I often felt like replying 'Up in a tree' or 'in a hut' rather than saying a six-bedroom mansion. Once I did say sarcastically that I lived in a tree, to be then asked how did you sleep at night to which I once replied 'by tying myself with a rope to a branch'. 'Did you have a bicycle to get around or did you walk to school?' to which I have jokingly replied 'I rode to school on an elephant'. However, I would mildly reply, 'I lived in a mansion and was chauffeured to school'. At other times I would be asked 'How did you come to be here?' I wanted to reply 'a great eagle brought me across the ocean or a whale dumped me on the beach' but said 'On a plane'. For those of you who say it is natural curiosity, I would like to you to understand that the questions not only showed ignorance and insularity but also a deep insensitivity which made me feel excluded – an outsider.

In this way, I was vaccinated by eating the bitter pill of humiliation, patronage and sometimes outright racism. I started slowly but my outrage at being 'dissed', patronised, discriminated against, being the object of both unconscious and conscious exclusion and racism started me on the path to becoming a strong, often fierce and definitely an independent woman. The change in my views and worldviews started imperceptibly but gained momentum as I went to work to make a living and to spending close to forty years in Australian corporate life.

Never again would I act with false modesty and be self-effacing. If someone started to patronise me or talked down to me (whatever their motivation) or make barely veiled racist remarks/questions, I would react with the fierceness of a guard dog. Along the way, I would give this advice to many south Asian people who came to Australia in the eighties, nineties and later:

> "If you behave like a smarmy puppy, wagging your tail
> and licking people's boots, the bully in some people

will cause them to kick you. Others may think you are
inferior and treat you as such. Learn to look people in
the eye and feel within you the pride and don't-mess-
with-me attitude of a German shepherd dog. Then
they will respect you and treat you like a person to
be reckoned with."

Recently I heard a presenter on Australian television talking to wives
of clergymen who had suffered domestic abuse including marital
rape. Those women were not prepared to show their faces and give
their true identities. I grieved with and for them because they seem
to have internalised the shame they suffered from their spouses. The
church hierarchy seemed to have little concern for many of these
women who now live in poverty, on single-parent pensions. Some of
them told horrifying stories of being hit, raped, choked, of watching
rage directed at their children who were beaten. Some were even
put outside the door, naked, in the middle of winter.

At least three of these women had clergymen husbands who studied
at a theological college where the women attended in a support
(!) role. They received instruction on how to be submissive and
supportive to their men.

It brought back many memories of my own first husband, who would
quote scripture to me, on my role as a wife and mother which was
an unreformed version of being a household-cum-sex slave. He
would instruct me in everything (as the 'head of the house') such as
grocery shopping, cooking, cleaning, ironing, folding and hanging
clothes, dishes and placing grocery tins in the pantry in a certain
order, dusting, toilet-paper use, sex, who to talk or not talk to, how to
greet him at the door every evening - by kneeling down and taking
his shoes off, gently taking his briefcase, serving him a cup of tea
and waiting while he drank it and later following him around as he

gave the 'white glove' treatment to the house. There was so much humiliation and infantilisation along with constant emotional, physical and financial abuse.

I could not talk to anyone because the elders of the church believed as he did and, as I found out years later, treated their wives similarly. I was expecting these men to help me and counsel him about his behaviour! Hah! Double hah! Why would they counsel him when they were doing the same themselves? I angered them when I brought my woes and tales of abusive behaviour to them. They would have had to counsel themselves and each other should their authenticity and human instincts caused them to look within and without. And the expected outcome and edict was: My husband was considered my 'lord' and I had to be submissive to him even though he could punch me and torture me mentally and emotionally by telling me details of my funeral or how he intended to snatch my daughter from me and run away to another country. Later I discovered that whenever an 'ism' or ideology including a religious one preaches superiority of one class over another it leads to excesses of control and domination, and sometimes, leads to violence.

The intergenerational trauma was to affect me as well. I was not stolen *per se* (like my grandmother whose remarkable story appears towards the end of this book) but I lost my social and cultural roots. In my home country, I was a woman of some social status and pedigree. I had lived a grand life and moved at the upper levels of intellectual, social and economic life. As the inheritor of a proud family tradition, I had the advantage of a university education, which at that time was still considered unusual, even though education, liberalism and free speech were a well-established tradition with the women in my family. However, in my new country, I was considered a woman who was a nobody – someone with little intellect, skills or social standing – with nothing to contribute.

My search for work was a shocking wake-up call to the realities of gender and ethnic equity. Having a college (undergraduate) degree from India meant nothing to potential employers in Australia. My view of myself as an educated, upper class woman was shattered. I was pushed to the bottom ranks of corporate life. In fact, my first job was as a casual farm labourer – gherkin-picking at $2 an hour. Soon after, I progressed to clerical work, doing typing and note-taking! I look back now and wonder about this single-minded focus on work and a career rather than applying for government aid for single mothers along with a subsidised Housing Dept. apartment as some of my friends urged me to do. But I had dreams of being a successful career woman, striding along men and women of similar education and worth, rather than availing myself of social security aid. Somehow being independent and resourceful was an instinctive choice I made and I have never regretted choosing that path.

I dredge up these memories and experiences now but for a long time I damped down and locked away those memories, emotions and thoughts in a recess in my head, heart and gut because to dwell on them brought bitter tears and deep pain. In the past few years, I have worked out why I buried the frustrations and anger to a deep level but at that time I believed I was lurching from one stage of life to another.

It was only in my thirties, after my first marriage ended, that I tuned into my thirst for knowledge and chose to do it by updating my academic skills. As my career struggles brought me into lower-level roles, I began to figure out how to gain a better way of being and living. I had to learn the hard way. I made my way to economic security and career progression via acquiring academic diplomas and degrees. I used tertiary education to jump-start my career and reaching the life I dreamt of. Thus I was able to use my own wits and intelligence to carve out a good life, a meaningful life. Was this a re-awakening of my feminine, clever self? Perhaps I was trying to recapture the emotional and intellectual highs I had enjoyed via academic success at matriculation and then my under-graduate degree. Education became the means of empowerment. Getting to the C-Suite or senior management team in corporations did not become an end in itself. Along the way I discovered my own inner values and principles of justice, compassion, equity which allowed me to make a change to my own and others' lives.

DARING TO DREAM

Australia was to be the making and re-making of me as a woman – liberated, emancipated, lively, socially active, career-oriented, ambitious, knowing that the world had no boundaries for me. This was the nineteen eighties and I was living at the junction of the new age of feminism, liberation and independence. Gaining personal freedom led to my awakening as a woman and human being.

I moved from the East and became a person of the West. I left behind a culture and tradition of paying respect to one's husband, family and elders to become one of the confident, individualistic people of western society. Well, not really, but I began to cultivate directness and straightforwardness as opposed to being humble and self-effacing. I stopped walking one step behind and forced myself to walk in the light, side by side with others. This took a long time in coming but is now ingrained – it is part of my very being.

When I first moved to Australia I naively thought that my race and gender would not be a problem in this democratic, equity-minded nation. I was blind to the effects my skin colour, race, ethnicity and gender would have in work places – including offices, training rooms and therapy clinics. Perhaps the origins of my 'blindness' lay in the liberal upbringing I had experienced, where girls received equal treatment in education and extra-curricular activities. The issues of ethnicity and gender were hidden within a fragile glass container of class and status derived from my parents' class, 'wealth' and the 'Anglophilia' embraced by an Indian oligarchic society.

There were some essential parts of my personality that helped me – my independence and need to have a voice, which had been stifled for close on ten years while I was married to an abusive, sexist and racist man. As a child and then as a teenager, I had been encouraged by my father and grandfather to be my own person, a human being with purpose with something to give to others.

I would later learn from my studies in psychotherapy and counselling that people have a locus of evaluation, or a value judgement, which can be external or internal. If we think of ourselves as oppressed or less-than-others, we may inadvertently cultivate what psychologists call an *external locus of control*. Such people feel that most of what happens to them is beyond their ability to influence and they 'introject' the values of significant others known during their growing-up years as well as those they learnt from their own society and culture. However, an individual with an *internal locus of evaluation* trusts their own instincts or their own organismic valuing process. They believe they can influence outcomes that affect them. They attribute success to their own efforts and abilities; they also expect to succeed, will be more motivated and more likely to learn.

Leaving my abusive husband was sad and painful, but ultimately redemptive. Looking back I can see the metamorphosis happening – little by little. I sought to become independent and look after my precious daughter, who would remain the sunshine and mainstay of my life. I took an administrative job to be near her, earn a living and bring about a stable foundation in our lives. At this time (age thirty), I also learnt to drive which was to increase my feelings of confidence and independence. The stability of having a tiny home – which I shared with the kind woman who had befriended me - became an anchor for me, a place to plant my feet in normality and go forward.

I worked for five or six years in this administrative role with about forty men, most of whom were kind and supportive of me. I was also unusual in my attitude to work as I took on more than I was supposed to do according to my job description. Work saved me. It gave me inner strength and a means of lifting my head up and showing myself to be strong, resourceful and willing to learn. It gave me dignity and freedom from being minimised and told I was good for nothing; it allowed me to regain my sanity and showcase my talent and skills.

STARING AT THE GLASS CEILING - DIRECT AND INDIRECT DISCRIMINATION

I began my corporate career in the late nineteen seventies. I was euphoric with my new found freedom – believing I could enter any field of endeavour that appealed to me, have equal access to any job for which I had qualifications and experience and the room to excel and shine in any industry or occupation that I chose to enter. I was sure I would no longer have to pretend to be 'less than' anyone else because of their fragile egos, traditions or fundamentalist doctrines.

I would soon learn that discrimination was alive and well.

Being poorly paid did not occur to me at that stage, but later on it would become an incentive and motivator to take action for myself and my sisters - women around me who were caught in the trap of female occupations which were paid below equivalent male occupations or in roles where men regularly earned or were paid more than the average women. Nor was I aware then of the glass ceilings, glass walls and the glass floor! That realisation would come soon enough – at that time, the euphoria of believing I had the freedom to study, work, and progress in a career as an equal human being was enough.

In the late 1960's, before I arrived in Australia, legislation had been passed to remove the 'marriage bar' in the Australian Public Service which forced women to leave work when they married. Later in 1975, Australia had passed the **Race Discrimination Act** and in 1984, Australia would get the **Sex Discrimination Act** which would prohibit discrimination on the basis of sex, marital or relationship status, actual or potential pregnancy, sexual orientation, gender identity etc in a range of areas of public life. In 1992, Australia would pass the **Disability Discrimination Act** which would be followed by the **Age Discrimination Act** IN 2004.

Notwithstanding all this legislation, things were far from equal for women. Equal pay for men and women had not come about despite passing various laws and the gap continues to this day (almost twenty years into the twenty-first century) despite much talk and encouragement to large corporations and smaller companies alike. In the late seventies-early eighties, certain occupations were still considered to be the domain of males and despite legislation would remain out of the reach of women for a few more decades. I had already been passed over or ignored for jobs for which I was well qualified within the organisation where I held an administrative role. Much of the experience could not be labelled direct discrimination; it was mostly systemic and indirect – for example, a deeply entrenched belief that only men could be managers or get promoted to certain ranks e.g. supervisors. Regulations still existed that stated that people under a certain height (say 172 cm or 5' 8") could not join the Police or Defence Forces.

Men who came after me in jobs were paid more than I had been because 'they were supporting families'. This was a throwback to the Harvester Case or a decision made in Australia in 1907 which decreed that a living wage considered "fair and reasonable" for an unskilled male should be sufficient for "a human being in a civilised community" to support a wife and children in "frugal comfort". Of course women were not covered by the basic wage and they continued to earn approximately half of male wages (54%) many years to come. Today the gap stands at 15%-17% on average when comparing male and female pay. Females were seen to be working for 'pin money' or to buy a few extra bits of luxury for their home – they were not seen to be breadwinners as I was often told by managers and recruiters. Many a time I retaliated by saying that I had a family to support and this was my sole source of income. However, the assumption was that all women had husbands earning the basic wage or that men with industrial and technical skills would be on a wage which was a few dollars higher. That women could be supporting themselves or a family on their own was disregarded. The worth of my work and whether I performed work of equal value was not taken into account. We were still second class citizens in terms of pay and equality of opportunity.

In the early eighties, when I was finally driven to study Human Resources and Organisation Development, I was also told by two supposed friends (white men in managerial roles) that I had two strikes against me – I was a woman (sexism) and coloured (racism). In fact, one of them made a Freudian slip when he saw me leaving the office to go on an errand. He yelled at me, 'Hey there chocolate chip' alluding to my nickname at that time but overtly corrected himself saying that he felt I was one of the best cookies in the cookie jar.

THROUGH GLASS CEILINGS AND DOORS – A CAREER IN HR MANAGEMENT

Why did I choose to go into Human Resources? I wanted to work with people and understand the ways good employment practices could help them at a personal and familial level. There is no doubt this was connected to my own experiences in finding work and climbing the career ladder. However, my immediate **non**-inspiration was the Vice-President of Human Resources in the organisation where I first found administrative work. Stories were told of his bullying and standover tactics towards unionised workers and his dismissive attitude to women. In my eyes he was also a blatant discriminator when it came to valuing men's and women's work in terms of pay, promotion and working conditions. He was scathing about women's worth and the occupations they were suited to working in. Other managers, who were ostensibly kind (read condescending) to women such as myself used his words and guidance to avoid promoting women or paying them at the same rate as men who did similar work. Their stock answer was: 'Women between twenty and forty get pregnant and hence training them is wasted!' It was considered a point of honour among the more traditional, hardline male managers to put down women who aspired to an education, or who came in as engineers or technical specialists, or those who wanted to be apprentices; their managerial style consisted of treating them like dirt or demeaning them, asking them to bring them cups of tea or file their papers or collect their dry-cleaning or order flowers for their wives - all the things which would prompt them to leave.

I think what drove me to study Human Resources and Organisation Development was a combination of positive role models in managerial and leadership behaviours that I had observed in my father and maternal grandfather and how they stacked up against the negative influence of this V.P. of HR and his outrageous behaviour. I knew what I wanted to do. Dismantle the practices and change the mindsets of men and systems like the ones he espoused. People like him did not know the meaning of equal employment opportunity or affirmative action or how to promote or attract qualified women into non-traditional roles. They did not realise the enormous benefits of extending the talent pool to include women and minority groups. Enrolling in the study of Human Resources and Organisation Development and aiming to get into this field was closely related to my readings in feminism, psychology, sociology and current affairs as well as personal life experiences in facing obstacles to having equitable and meaningful work.

The positive exemplar in Human Resources was my maternal grandfather (see his story at the end of this book), who was the Personnel & Welfare Manager for one of the large textile corporations in northern India. He cared about workers and intervened on their behalf with the owners and managers; he set up structures such as schools for workers and childcare for their children; he had low-rent accommodation built for workers along with after-hours gyms; he installed rehabilitation programs for injured workers to learn new skills and overcome the psychological and physical traumas of their injuries. He intervened with managers and directors on behalf of men and women who were considered to be at the bottom of the heap. He was and is my inspiration.

The other positive role model was my father. I remembered and learnt from the many instances of leadership skills he had displayed as a military officer, his care for organisation and internal processes based on rationality and his passion for soldiers' welfare. I believed he was the epitome of a person with a successful career, a man who came from obscurity to become a high-ranking officer all because of his self-confidence, his will to succeed and his insatiable ability to learn.

I have often wondered why I did not go into other roles which could have taken me away from corporate life. One such was a teaching qualification which I could have undertaken at that time after completing a couple of years at Teachers' College. Perhaps, being a single mother with a child to support was against me because I would have to give up my job and survive on a scholarship if any was available. I did contemplate it for a while. I also thought about entering the government ranks i.e. the Public Service at State level, but decided against this route. In hindsight, I should have done so as to have an effect at policy and program level. Later, as my social activism came to the fore, I would turn my attention to working in not-for-profit and non-government organisations voicing concerns and laying out factual materials which have an impact on policy.

It seems entering organisational or corporate life at that time was the closest I could come to following in my father's and grandfather's footsteps and creating the life I had once known.

My qualifications from a non-Australian university were not going to help me as Australia did not recognise degrees from other countries. So even if it meant taking a step backwards, I decided to do a degree which would be useful in jump-starting a career. This was 1981 and the academics at the College/ University that I applied to said they would let me in 'conditionally' – I could stay if I could keep up with the rigours of academic study during the first semester. I was the only woman in a class of over twenty men. My life changed from working hard during the day and then spending the evenings with my daughter. Now I would go straight to university two to three nights a week from my full-time job to attend classes and lectures, using the weekends to complete assignments, while my dear ten-year old daughter was cared for by my kind house-mate and child-carer. Not only was I the only female in the class but also the student who excelled in every subject, managing to do three subjects in the first semester, earning high distinctions in each. After this semester, I did not hear a word about my 'conditional' acceptance into the course.

One of the subordinates of the not-so-wonderful V.P. of Human Resources also went to night classes with me. I was then in my mid-thirties; one evening as we walked back to our cars he told me that I was too old to ever make it into Human Resources! I was shocked at his sexist and ageist remarks. In anger, I yelled at him but he said he was telling me the truth (his truth, I think)! A couple of years ago, I contacted him through Facebook and reminded him of his remarks. He had the grace to say 'Shame on me'. The world and his own personal circumstances had changed over the intervening thirty years, bringing him to a realisation of his hurtful and prejudicial words.

A SECOND MARRIAGE TO FIND PERSONAL HAPPINESS

As I was finding my feet in my professional career, I met another man and after having a few years as a single parent I married again. He was very handsome but not emotionally available, more in love with his mother than with me – though at times his words seemed to convey a dislike of her and feeling that she was a burden. Why did I once again marry a man who disliked his mother just as my first husband had? What was the shadow part of me that I was working out? Did I dislike myself as a mother? Or did I dislike my mother and was trying to distance myself from her? Did I feel guilt in my soul for not having provided my daughter with an idyllic family life and a mother who was there to fuss over her and give her cookies and milk when she came home from school?

I once compared my second husband to an oil painting of a handsome man, great for my parlour wall, but unable to function as a full human being in a relationship and give of himself psychologically and emotionally. Later, I said to a close friend, 'I may as well have bought an annual ticket to the Art Gallery as have him in my life'. We could not connect or share intimate talk. His first priority was his mother and that was deeply damaging to our relationship. I think he saw me as a mother-figure and was taken by my exotic, good looks and I was indulgent enough to let him go his own way.

And racism again came into the picture again because he and his mother felt the need to keep me under their collective thumbs! I did not have equal rights in that family – I would not be consulted on where to live or how to spend funds which we had both contributed to - even though I had been living in this country, been a career woman and an achiever in academic life for over ten years by that time.

I believe much of that situation is my fault. I had not yet worked out my own path and destiny. I had not worked out what I truly deserved in an intimate personal relationship. I had not become differentiated from my own family of origin and was still looking for someone to rescue me. I was to learn later on, when I started studying psychotherapy, how and why relationships are so challenging. We all bring our own backed up 'crap' or dysfunctionality into a relationship. And if we have not worked out our own values, what has led to the way we behave, what we want out of a relationship, our own personality quirks (including our hot buttons), our ways of relating, and reached some level of individuation and differentiation, then that relationship will not succeed.

It is said that differentiation is 'the process of becoming different by growth or development'. And while my academic and professional knowledge had grown, I had not yet reached emotional and psychological development and growth.

FOLLOWING MY DREAM - ROADBLOCKS AND CHAMPIONS IN CORPORATE LIFE

By this time, I was beginning to learn how to read people and their motives correctly. Some managers had held me back despite my single-minded focus on learning and excelling in my job and the hard work I was prepared to put in. They used me to further their own promotions and careers. Many made advances and wanted me sexually, and yet others were afraid of me. Others were too traditional in their outlook and refused to accept that my hard work and intelligence could be parlayed into promoting me into a better organisational position or a supervisory or managerial role. All this said, there were some men at work respected me and were willing to take a chance on promoting me and growing my talents and skills.

A colleague in the department where I had my first administrative assistant job told me years later of an incident that happened in the early 1980's; a delegation composed of ten men in his section went to their manager when their supervisor was leaving. They said that they had found that I had picked up and learnt the work done by their supervisor easily and seamlessly, and wanted the manager to appoint me to the supervisory role. Their argument was cogent and reasonable but their (white) manager yelled at them, 'I am not going to have a woman supervise men. I will look for someone else.' None of them had the heart to tell me of this incident at the time. Sexism, and to some extent racism, had won because I was probably the only woman of colour in that organisation at that time.

More examples of racism abound. There was another man whom I dreaded; he always accosted me in a filing room which had only one entry – he would put his arms out, trying to grab me as he blocked the doorway of the room and leer at me saying 'Darling, let's have an Asian affair', referring to a popular travel advertisement at that time. Others would use my intellect and skills to write erudite reports which came from them, or get insights and deep knowledge, then frame it as their own, without giving me credit or promoting me to a position which carried a title and benefits. Even after having received a promotion to a responsible role, I would discover that the demeaning behaviour did not diminish or stop.

Among these dismissive men was a managerial and technological dinosaur, who suspected any one particularly a woman who had risen by dint of hard work to be a Production Planner a role which included industrial engineering, metal resourcing and production output . Every half hour he would march up and down the pathway past my desk to see what I was doing, gaze at my computer and papers on my desk and ask twenty questions... not of support but to trip me up. I must admit that I got my own back in subtle and not-so-subtle ways with the help of a young male colleague e.g. linking together all the paper clips in his bowl, hiding his telephone in a bottom drawer of his desk and then ringing him, upsetting the order in which his pencils were kept (pointy side to the window). He was not on his own in the sexist behaviour he displayed, which was more suited to the factory slaves at the start of the Industrial Revolution.

Amidst all the discrimination and lack of credit and being treated like a second-class worker, there were some positive experiences during those tough early years. Along with the 'put-downers', I also had the privilege of working with men who were early champions of change and helped me climb 'the corporate ladder'.

In the early 1980's, two men in particular recognised my talents. And they would be instrumental in helping me make the leap from an administrative role into working at a level more suited to my skills.

After five or six years in the Administrative and Technical Assistant job where I took on and performed additional duties as a laboratory supervisor, I applied for and got a promotion to the role of production planner. The manager of a large Planning department recognised my skills and learning abilities. It was a role which would require a sort of apprenticeship, learning to liaise with and understand Sales and Marketing requirements, translate them to the Factory to discover if we could make such material and study Industrial Engineering to work out how. No woman had ever been hired for the role because it involved machine and metal knowledge which in those days was a 'male only' area.

Nevertheless he interviewed me. During my interview, I said I had noticed that some of the men doing the production planning role were not technically qualified but had applied themselves to learn mechanical, production and sales liaison skills. I also said, rather vaingloriously, that I believed that I was an intelligent woman (meaning more than averagely intelligent!) and so whatever an average man could do I could do too. Famous last words!

He decided to take a chance on me, saying he had noticed my diligent and earnest application and believed I could transfer that attitude to a role where knowledge and expertise came through apprenticeship. I proved to be an earnest and willing student on the job and my teacher was a kind and gentle man whose only shortcoming was that he smoked incessantly (in the days where you could smoke in open offices). Within six months, I was not only doing the job I was promoted to do, but doing it very well.

Around this time, I started studying for my Human Resources degree and had begun to enjoy the challenges of organisational psychology, employment law, team and individual performance, and most of all organisational culture. The more I studied the more I realised that studying something I loved made me better at it – and of course I had an end goal in mind.

It was the mid-nineteen-eighties when a second man, the Chief Executive Officer of the organisation, came along to help me. In my eagerness I had blathered to him in the cafeteria about my studies and what I hoped to accomplish. Twelve months later I received a call from his personal assistant to come and see him. I had forgotten about my euphoric words in the cafeteria and went into his office on shaky knees. I was convinced he was going to fire me! He told me that he had a vacancy on the Organisation Development team which required company knowledge and skills as well as formal Human Resources and Organisational Psychology knowledge and he couldn't think of a better candidate than myself. I was bowled over and tottered out of his office on even shakier legs.

But my 'elevation' to 'managerial' or professional status made many people envious or dismissive of my skills and how I got a higher level role. Shortly after getting the promotion, one man chose to follow the course of disrespect and devaluation. I met him on a social golf occasion when I was with my partner and he had his wife in tow. He chose to introduce me with an off-hand remark 'she is the little typist from the Planning office'. I was appalled, dumbfounded and tongue-tied. I did not know how to hit back at him and call him a demeaning, sexist coward for failing to acknowledge my skills and my rise to managerial status.

A few years later in another organisation, I came across a CEO who held very 'old-fashioned' views about managerial prerogative. He believed he had the right to do as he wished in selecting, promoting and rewarding people. He decided to reward a couple of men at a certain organisational level with company cars, considering them job status rewards and dismissing women at the same level and rank (including myself) who were performing vital work with similar if not higher responsibility, as not deserving to have this reward. I received a couple of complaints from women who saw this injustice. I went to see him to get him to reverse this decision or reward people at that organisational level including women with a company benefit. It was also not in line with company policy as laid down by head office or employment agreements made with the men and women in these job classifications. Disdainfully, he cited his 'managerial prerogative'. Knowing he was a good Christian man, I could not help myself and said, 'well that is both against the law of the land and the law of god'. His office door slammed shut in my face. The phone began to ring as I reached my office and people enquired if I had been fired. I replied I could not be fired for speaking the truth. Eventually, head office came down in favour of keeping legislation and providing equal rewards but it was done silently and 'confidentially' without any apology or reference to the injustice done for the past few months. I earned the CEO's permanent wrath for pointing out what was both a breach of internal policy and discrimination law but my forthright words and actions meant that my own rewards in that organisation were minimal from that time onward.

After moving into Human Resources and Organisation Development, I discovered that Australia ranked almost at the bottom of OECD (Organisation for Economic Cooperation and Development) nations in terms of occupational sex segregation – and professions such as teaching, nursing, human resources and counselling are still considered feminised. On a personal level, issues and conflicts posed by my gender and racial or ethnic background have frequently surfaced over the years, both verbally and non-verbally, in a potent and sometimes shocking fashion. Being a woman was enough in the latter half of the twentieth century and even at the beginning of the twenty-first century to prevent you from breaking through the glass ceiling or glass walls, but imagine the plight of a migrant woman, particularly one of colour!

ROLE MODELS FOR WOMEN OF COLOUR

It took me twenty years to get from being a poor single parent to entering the Executive level and becoming the CEO of a small not-for-profit organization. I made the journey without any role models, mentors or guides as I navigated my way in a white, male-dominated world. I aligned my mental compass and leadership role models with those of my father and grandfather and those 'white' males who had behaved with respect and held the internal values of equity and honesty. I had begun to absorb western values of individuality, forthrightness, love of equality and justice. Unconsciously or consciously, I role-modelled myself on the men and women who showed respect and welcomed me as an equal. I am glad they were there for me giving me friendship and a leg up the ladder because I showed skills, intelligence and good values similar to their own.

I have begun to understand that individuals from minority groups, whose culture is different from the dominant group, begin to differentiate themselves from their own cultural or gender group and act more like people from the dominant culture. Not because these individuals (wrongly) feel inferior and less deserving. Women of colour who find themselves in a leadership role have to grapple with a complexity of personal emotions, a need to overcome subtle and not-so-subtle stereotypical messages regarding womanhood and race (beamed by the white male-dominated society around them) as well as their own cultural upbringing. This was my situation for many years as I sought to be authentic yet relevant to people on my team and organisation.

The difficulties facing migrant and refugee women is recognised by champions of Human Rights. They say it is not enough to just promote the participation of women in economic life as if all women are part of one composite and homogenous group. Race and gender intersect to create disadvantage and discrimination for migrant and refugee women as they try to participate in and not only get the benefits of employment but also prosper and advance their lives and careers. The disadvantage faced by migrant women is multi-faceted and new strategies are required to give a voice to their particular experiences and many different avenues explored to give them the space to aspire and to reach areas and positions hitherto shut to them.

I discovered that the community and society I have lived in is moving but far too slowly. To give you a some examples: I have been stopped on a few occasions by the police because I drove a new-model car because it had been provided by my organization or I had purchased it Once I was stopped as I drove in rural NSW, Australia, with a 'white' friend in the passenger seat and questioned about my movements. We had stopped for lunch in a country town, then driven on to call on some friends and not finding them home, decided to look at the sights before returning. Apparently, this was interpreted as 'loitering' or 'casing various premises' with a view to burglary. Other times, the person in the passenger seat has was deemed to be the legitimate owner of the car and I was questioned but assumed to be the hired driver. Another time recently, I was stopped, asked to get out of the car and questioned to find out if that was my own car and if so, where had I got it from. Obviously, my colour and gender was against me.

Many times, I have been dismissed by sales assistants either from upmarket boutiques, jewellery shops or car-yards because they have assumed that as a woman of colour, I could not afford to buy a new model car or a piece of jewellery or a new outfit. If I have not been overtly dismissed, I am followed around the store in case I shoplift some of their precious goods. In one case, the female owner of a TV and white-goods outlet told the mortified shop assistant not to bother to serve me as it would not be worth it. I walked out without buying but told many of my friends about the discourteous behaviour. I remember my Marketing 101 principle: a person having one great experience of customer service will tell ten people; a person with a dreadful customer service experience tells thirty others.

To get over the car sales problem, I used to take male friends along whom salesmen (yes mostly men) would latch on to. The salesmen would give them their best sales talk and most attractive deals. My male friends would reiterate that I was the buyer, but the salesmen would continue to work on the males, selling them the car's qualities and offering them the opportunity to drive. Needless to say, if I find I am dismissed or treated as a 'nobody' because of my skin colour or ethnicity, I move on because I believe such people do not need to get my money!

This lack of role models for women of colour became a current flowing unconsciously in my psyche. It reached its full manifestation in my senior years inspiring my advocacy work with Aboriginal and multi-cultural women and those affected by domestic violence

THE 21ST CENTURY BUT THE DIRT (COLOUR) STILL WON'T WASH OFF

From the very start of my working life in a lowly paid administrative job and later while I studied for a career to increase my prosperity and standing, I began to wonder why going up the ladder was so difficult. I wondered if some of my differences - looks, ambition, confidence, education - were so conspicuous and egregious that people (by that I mean the white men and women who govern corporate Australia) did not want to hire me because I would not fit into that wonderful word they often use and still use about their organisation: 'our culture'. I would fret after each blow or 'kiss-off' to my wafer-thin ego and promise myself to keep my 'differences' under wraps, and pretend to be 'whiter than white' next time, and all would be well.

Did it get better? A little bit here and there but overall the ladder to success has been difficult. I have persisted despite any subtle or overt discrimination that may have existed on the basis of my gender and race. If I was not wanted, I would tell myself that they did me a favour as working with discriminatory or prejudiced people would have made my life miserable. However, the upshot is that I have become stronger, more confident, more resilient, and more knowledgeable about my role, and the intrinsic 'power of my personality' has started to shine through. I have also had the great privilege of working with good white men and women - Australian,

British, American, European - who believed in me and encouraged me to climb the career ladder. They seem to have judged my skills and experience as 'meritorious'. This term is often used in corporate life but simply means that the standards set by the people on top are used to judge the ones coming up. Such standards may not necessarily be relevant to the role or the organisation or reflect the zeitgeist of our times.

Despite all the roadblocks, I persisted. I continued in Human Resources successfully getting roles in the pharmaceutical, consulting and manufacturing industries. Along the way, I upgraded my qualifications and acquired a Masters of Commerce (Employment Relations) again via part-time study while I worked full-time. Shortly after finishing this degree, I saw a need to add to my knowledge of Organisational Psychology in order to support women and men in both personal and organisational matters. My personal attitude and desire to provide a fair and just playing field in organisations had led to employees trusting me and coming to me for 'advice' in matters which affected them – personal stress, disputes with managers, wanting a fair outcome as they navigated company and legislative matters. The CEO of the organisation I worked in began to refer to the people wanting to see me on a variety of matters as my 'surgery'! This led me begin studying Psychotherapy and Counselling, obtaining a Graduate Diploma in 1999. I also began going for personal therapy which was unheard of in Australia at that time. But this was to be the making and reinventing of me. It would help me to understand myself and the purpose of my own life but it would also equip me to become a vital right-hand person to CEO's and senior managers as we wrestled with the ups-and-downs of organisational culture and why people at various organisational levels behaved in response to restructuring, redundancy and take-overs. This attempt to make sense of my own life and understand people better helped me to reach the C-Suite in organisations. It also laid the foundation for me to teach, consult and coach later in a semi-retired life.

The higher I climbed the corporate ladder, I encountered yet more examples of racism and discrimination. I was always respectful to my team or the staff who reported to me who in turn were loyal and devoted to me. However, I would discover time and again that external associations and their representatives, fellow managers and administrative staff in other organisations would demean me. As a General Manager or Director of Human Resources, I travelled regularly for work, sometimes with one or two team members. When arriving at our hotel or motel, I would discover that members of my staff or the consultant I had hired to run a training workshop would get the large front-facing rooms and I would be relegated to the littlest maid's room at the back of the hotel next to the cleaning closet. Often my staff and colleagues would be embarrassed for me and insist that we swop rooms which I refused to do. This happened too many times for it to be considered a coincidence.

In one particular case, I had decided to hold a workshop with my team, who came from around the country, at a hotel close to the ocean. We came in one afternoon and each one received their room allocation. Most of the team were assigned rooms on the fifth and sixth floors facing the water. I was assigned a room upstairs at the back overlooking the alley with garbage dumpsters. The carpet had water-damage and the fittings in the room and bathroom were old and discoloured. I went downstairs to Reception and asked if I could have a better room, a different one, preferably facing the water. I was told 'Certainly, but you will have to pay more for it. Do you have a personal credit card you can use?' My Administrative assistant, who was standing by my side, yelled 'What?' and almost leapt across the counter to accost the receptionist. With a gesture, I held her back. The reception staff had assumed that this woman with dark skin standing in front of them was the Administrative assistant and all my white colleagues and staff were my managers and superiors. My Assistant was to have the last word anyway when she replied: 'Yes she is our boss. She has a company card which she will use to pay for all of us'. I got a room change but no apology.

On another occasion, I travelled interstate to one of the company's manufacturing sites. I endured many dismissive looks and various forms of demeaning behaviour but told myself to 'stop being fragile' and take them in my stride. That evening, I was invited to attend a sales conference which would be attended by over fifty people. The Sales Manager of the group organisation, who was a few rungs below me on the organisation chart, got up and gave his motivational talk and then introduced me to the gathered staff by saying 'I am pleased to introduce the HR Director. If you want to meet her, just look for a black face with white teeth and you will know who she is'. Needless to say there was an audible hush in the room. I turned to look at the local Human Resources Manager who had bowed his head in embarrassment and covered his face with his hands. Again, trying to take it in my stride, I smiled and waved and decided to brush it off as another example of backwoods 'redneck' behaviour. However, the news travelled to the head office faster than I did. My CEO at the Head Office confronted me the same week by asking why I had not reported this to him. I demurred by saying 'Oh, I am used to it'. He insisted that the Sales Manager who made the remark and the V.P. of Sales to whom this man reported – both apologise to me. Cold comfort I say when the damage had been done.

Travelling in my corporate job as HR Director was the norm. Every other week found me jetting to various capital cities and a couple of times a year overseas. I was used to the travel, the nuances and difficulties at various airports in most cities. I also discovered as security became a major issue at airports that the screening process was very racially skewed. I had dark skin and steel replacements in both knees which meant I was always led aside and patted down assiduously. Very often this patting down was combined with having my hand baggage tested for traces of explosives. However, I did not have facial hair, so begrudgingly I was allowed through.

In the late nineties, I was travelling to London to attend a work conference and had a business class ticket. After getting through the body scans and pat downs, I approached the business class ticket line. The airline staff, however, waved me away and told me to go to the economy queue. Several times, I held my paper-ticket out in front of me but they would not deign to look at the ticket or my 'dark' face. Finally, I went to the economy queue in an attempt to get on to the flight and was queried by the staff in the economy lane, who said: 'Madam, you have a Business class ticket, why don't you go into that queue?' So I told them my sad story and one of them accompanied me to the Business Class queue and helped me to get on board with my valid ticket!! I am still a great supporter of this airline but this was not to be the end of it.

A few years later, I was waiting in the airline's airport club for a return plane home. I approached the barman for a drink and found myself second in the queue. After serving the man ahead of me, the barman looked over my head to the man behind me and asked 'What would you like, sir?' The man was puzzled and insisted that I was before him in the line for drinks but the barman kept insisting and asking for his order. Obviously my dark skin meant I was invisible! I turned to the man in the queue and said 'please order or we will be here all night!' He did and then the barman with a sardonic raise of his eyebrow looked at me. I gave him my order and disdainfully he poured me a glass of wine. I have wondered if he treated all 'darkies' like this; likely the darkies like me were invading the sacred premises of the club to get their free grog before they lay down on the carpet and started spewing and snoring!! I complained to the supervisor on duty that day at the airline club but she was very defensive and kept saying that the barman must be tired etc. No apology was forthcoming. I told my CEO, a man of great principle, three months after I returned from this trip; he was furious and wanted to write to the airline and complain of their racism and rudeness.

I have seen that white Australia would not open its doors to me willingly. Yes, I know some of the barriers are unconscious at times but so many high-level managers refuse to believe in unconscious bias. Corporate Australia would let men of lesser talent rise to the top of the career pile rather than give women like me a chance. This was brought home to me yet again a few years after I completed a Masters degree in Commerce and had twenty years of high-level experience. One of my fellow female students and I unknowingly applied for the same job. Neither of us was successful in getting the role but we later discovered that the person with the lowest scores and wits in our Masters program got the job because he was a male and they wanted to preserve that male, macho environment!

The double jeopardy of sexism and racism has been compounded by ageism. I have found myself in interviews for top Human Resources and General Management roles with recruiters who have skirted the issue of race and colour and gender, sometimes using vague words about culture and team spirit to give me the brush-off. Others have tried to trick me during interviews to ask my age believing that if they confronted a person in the middle of an interview you may reveal your age unwittingly.

On one occasion I was interviewed by a well-known international head-hunting organisation where the recruiting manager asked me point-blank: 'How old are you?' I remonstrated by saying that the information was irrelevant, but he hassled and cornered into give him an answer. Another head-hunter pursued the same question; I got the better of him by scribbling in a wrong date on the form and then crossing it off. Apparently, he relayed the misinformation to my future CEO boasting about his cleverness. The CEO, to his great credit, warned the recruiter that he was on fragile ground with his sexist and ageist tactics and should he persist in this course he would never get another recruitment job out of him again. I was to have a great corporate relationship and friendship with this particular CEO. He was one of the good white men who believed in me which I believe were due to a synchronicity of values – honesty, transparency and straight-talking.

RACISM AND SEXISM IN EVERYDAY LIFE

The coming of the twenty-first century has not brought equity and a level playing field. Over the past ten to fifteen years I have experienced more racism and discrimination than I have during my entire forty-five years in Australia. Some has been so blatant as to be breath-taking. I was on the board of directors of a small community organisation whose manager (a white man) openly declared to members of the community cooperative that he would make sure to get rid of me from the board of directors. What was his reason? Perhaps because I did not pander to his nepotism and lack of governance knowledge. He had hired a crony of his to come on to the board and did not see it as a conflict of interest. It was also known that he had dismissed a female consultant the year before because he did not like people of her race (Asian). It seemed he was not only racist but also sexist and made it his business to bully, harass and push two other women out of their roles on the board. Finally, I made a complaint in writing to the Registrar of not-for-profit companies, which was supported and substantiated by a founder-member of the community group, who had heard and witnessed this manager's words. Two other directors supported me but the complaint was fobbed off for weeks and the final message received was that I should pursue it through legal means.

Discrimination and racism is not just to be found in the top-end of corporate Australia nor on not-for-profit boards! I have come across racist, demeaning aggressions by members of the caring professions. Their superciliousness, patronage and racism knows no bounds. Five years ago, I went to my local medical centre to see a doctor. I discovered that the Practice Manager (a young white woman) had decided to change the rules. Being the new broom that was sweeping clean, she had decided to make to make the centre more efficient by not allowing patients to 'hang' around the waiting room. When I entered and asked for my usual doctor, she barked at me, to make an appointment and come back. I did but would have to come back an hour later. I pleaded: 'Could I wait to see any other doctor please because I am really ill.' She said: 'You can't sit here. You have an appointment (an hour away) so go away and come back.' I knew I would have to sit in the car in the parking area or wait outside on the cold street. 'Can't I sit here till then? We have always sat here and waited for the next available doctor', I said. 'Has something changed?' She raised her voice: 'No, you are not allowed to sit here. Go away till your appointment is due and then come back'.

Unfortunately, it caused me to go into my 'consultant' mode and ask if this was in keeping with the vision and aims of the Centre and the Hippocratic oaths of the doctors who worked there. The woman's voice which had been rising for a while now reached a shout and she told me to get out and come back some other time. One of the senior doctors stepped out, stood next to me and asked her "What's the matter?" and she replied that 'this woman (meaning me) is making problems'. The doctor immediately replied 'Tell the woman to go away'. No question of asking me as I sat two feet away from him as he stood in his doorway as to what I wanted and what was wrong. The woman's defensiveness and rudeness coupled with the doctor's rude response, referring to me as if I was an inconvenient bit of trash in the centre, caused me to leave the centre. The next day, after making another appointment, I went to see my usual doctor who proceeded to 'counsel' me and tell me that he had received a complaint about me from these two people. And no, he did not wish to hear my side of the story. Another receptionist who had been present in the surgery was to tell me some months later that if they had asked her, she would have told them who was shouting and complaining. Now when I go to the medical centre I try to creep in hoping the 'nasty' doctor will not be there. I feel traumatised when I do bump into him on the premises because he glares and stares and snarls at me. I wish in hindsight I had complained to the Health Commission about this behaviour. They seem to have forgotten their Hippocratic (or is it hypocritical?) oath and behave as if patients are there to be vilified, patronised and mistreated because of the medicos' god-given white superiority.

I have been 'dissed' or put down, not just by ignorant and uneducated men and women, but also by educated feminist women. I keep wondering if this stereotyping based on race and skin colour has changed over the past twenty years? Not really. At a women's discussion forum recently, I observed the president of the feminist group that I belong to introduce a couple of women from a sister organisation. One of the women being introduced was of east-Asian origin and the other was a white woman. The president of my group introduced the white woman as the manager of the sister organisation and the woman of east Asian origin as her assistant. Wrong, wrong, wrong. It was the other way around. We still have not learnt the perils of stereotyping – that we make assumptions based on our unconscious biases and beliefs.

On another occasion, I was invited to join a committee of women engaged in tertiary education. At one planning meeting, we went around the room volunteering to do certain jobs, outlining areas where we could add value because of our personal skills and areas of interest. I volunteered to help another woman in the marketing space, editing and re-casting documents for sharing with our membership. At lunch-time, the President jotted down the names of those who had volunteered and the roles they were prepared to work in. When it came to the marketing and editing of documents, she put down the first woman's name and forgot to mention me. I gently reminded her.

At the end of the afternoon, the same thing happened – jobs and people were matched up and noted down and again she chose to 'forget' me. I had had enough by then and asked if my 'dark' face had made me invisible or somehow precluded me from adding value in the marketing and editing role. She said she had forgotten – a second time! Perhaps she may not have known that I had received distinctions in my undergraduate degree in English Literature. Her unconscious had played its part in stereotyping and dismissing me. My brown skin meant that I could not possibly know enough English or engage in editing and formulating vital documents!

I have experienced this form of unconscious discrimination several times over the years. Many have not recognised my prowess or command of the English language. Perhaps some judge me by their own lack of skills or knowledge of grammar, punctuation, syntax, phonics and spelling. In one instance, I was in a sitting room with four women friends who were doing a crossword puzzle, yelling out to each other and reading out clues but never did they include me. They yelled out each other's names – all except mine. Their demeanour and words showed they were excluding me – and this reflected their deeply held (unconscious), stereotypical beliefs about people of colour. Perhaps my dark skin precluded me from knowing and being proficient in the English language. Yet I was the only one in the group who regularly did cryptic crosswords and is part of another group who SMS each other regularly when they are stumped by clues.

I have also been at women's clubs and sometimes feminist gatherings, where I have been treated as if I was invisible. I see women entering the group or sitting next to or opposite me wish other women in the group good day and start up a conversation, but ignore me. Perhaps my dark skin makes them uncomfortable or makes me invisible even in bright light! At other times, I have heard women of colour or various ethnicities described by their skin colour and facial features and patronising remarks such as 'bright colours look so good on you black girls'. I think they believe they are being complimentary but I feel like a specimen or an organ-grinder's monkey dressed up in a velvet skirt! I feel patronised. I want to ask if that is all we are i.e. women of colour, to be described superficially without any allusion or noticed paid to our intelligence, wit, skills, or other 'hidden' qualities.

Sadly I have discovered that not all women deplore sexism and various forms of sexual harassment. Recently I was amazed to hear an older woman complain that she missed whistles, catcalls and remarks from men on construction sites because it made her 'feel young and attractive'. Well, I am glad they don't whistle and make rude remarks as a woman walks by. A recent video made and publicised by a women's organisation shows how women feel in danger and uncomfortable with catcalls and comments from men and one in three women feel frightened when they have that experience. Men have learned the hard way about respecting women as the media stars around the world have learnt through the #MeToo movement. I am glad such behaviour is on the decline and in time will stop altogether. In general, women have learnt faster than men because they have had their own experiences to draw on. Women have not rushed out to ogle men in tight jeans or grab them by their crotches because they were turned on by their clothing or demeanour. Women have had concepts of respect drummed into them from childhood by their immediate family members and certainly through their socialisation.

Recounting such experiences, I feel that the change in corporate and social life is still to come. I believe I have worked and studied diligently most of my life and have always wanted a job or promotion on my merits. Getting into plum jobs was difficult but I did not allow this to hold me back. I climbed the corporate ladder using my knowledge and skills in my chosen field. At the time I started my journey in the mid-nineteen-eighties, men were still at the forefront in the Human Resources field though women were beginning to be seen at various levels. I used all the people and culture strategies I knew as well as putting in processes and systems to work with executive teams to differentiate the organisation from its peers. With staff within the organisation, I worked using motivational and positive psychology, a raft of organisation change management strategies, team and individual plans for learning and development, remuneration linked to performance, goal-oriented personal development strategies, succession planning, workplace wellness and employee assistance programs among a host of initiatives to keep staff motivated and productive. Once I got through the interview door, I made friends with fellow executives and staff at all levels of the organisation to make it a friendly place. One of my first rewards in the early nineteen nineties was to receive awards from the Business Council of Australia and Business Review Weekly for being 'A Family Friendly company' (long before this became the norm), 'Using strategic initiatives as a small to medium size employer', plus awards for equal employment opportunity (now part of the Diversity and Inclusion space) and the Prime Minister's Award for employing people with a disability. However, studying psychotherapy and counselling not only brought the most meaning to my life it also added depth and understanding to the initiatives and insights I used in working with the Chief Executive officer and members of the executive team.

Experiences like mine abound. Till today, professional women will tell you that they are treated like assistants to the white male in the room. Many professional women are still asked to fetch the coffees or glasses of water. They get allocated the worst places around the table. They are looked at with a barely concealed sneer or disdainful or exasperated looks which seem to say: 'What would you know?' Most often they are patronised and talked down to... I almost expect a large hand to come out and pat me on the head with words like 'well done, dearie' or 'is that all you have to say, girlie?'

However, I stayed on the learning curve realising that there were some things I could get away with, but at a huge cost of marginalisation, misrepresentation and disempowerment. So I have gradually developed a two-pronged strategy in my professional and personal relationships.

Usually I start by using my intellect, expertise and verbal skills. I have never used my appearance or sexuality even as a good-looking young woman. (Perhaps because I was unaware of its impact; more likely due to my innate pride in my intelligence and knowledge.) My persona seems to change as I become comfortable in the work place. I begin neutralising the 'double jeopardy' I experience by becoming larger than life – voicing my beliefs passionately and displaying a colourful identity alongside my professional skills and mental acuity. I have succeeded by doing this to a large extent, although I have reflected many times that, while I have always needed to 'work twice as hard as a man and been three times more loyal than a dog', I still could not reach the top echelons of an organisation. The subtle but condescending remarks and various unconscious behaviours and attitudes connected to sexism and racism affected my psyche and have saddened and embittered me on various occasions.

I am glad to say that not all men and women are sexist or racist. I am thankful to the many kind people who have helped and befriended me. Shortly after finishing my first degree in counselling and psychotherapy, I met my life partner at a somatic therapy workshop. We worked well together through the various exercises and role-plays set for us. We exchanged business cards – mine gave my role in a big corporate; his card showed his name and underneath his title 'Human Being'. I was both delighted and impressed. A few days later we met for coffee where we chatted about various things. At one stage I remarked ...'god knows what will happen'... to which he replied 'whatever she thinks'. I was amazed and delighted to find a man who could possibly think that god could be female or have female qualities. This led to a good friendship and we have been life partners for almost twenty years now. By his words and actions, he makes me believe that good people, people conscious of the effects of racist and sexist behaviours, people of compassion and kindness exist everywhere.

DOUBLE WHAMMY AND THE NEW GENERATION

My daughter who came to Australia as an eight-month old baby has had a few brushes with racism. Neither of us has thought it was blatant or that our friends would make racist remarks perhaps out of some unconscious bias or stereotypical views. She was stepping out of the shower, after a session at a day spa where she had been with a couple of friends. One of her companions remarked as she came out 'Hey, the dirt is not off yet'! My daughter grinned in embarrassment at her friend's unconsciously racist remarks, far too taken aback to tell her to 'get lost'. Needless to say, the friendship died soon after.

A little while ago, she came across it again while working as a project manager in a large organisation. When asked by her boss why she could not work on a Sunday which was Mothers' day, my daughter replied that she would be dining with me. The reply came 'Oh have a great curry!' Well meant no doubt, but it left my daughter speechless, totally taken aback. The implicit bias, the stereotype had slipped out and draped itself over this highly educated person's perceptions. Unconscious bias is part of this implicit thinking of which gender, race and ageist thoughts and stereotypes are sub-branches. Remember not just sexist or racist people have unconscious biases. In fact, most of us fair, human, equitable people have blind spots and some of these blind spots are about race, religion, gender.

She has also had her fair share of 'where are you from?' questions which sometimes bewilder her and other times rouse her ire. She came here as a baby, grew up and went to school here and has always thought of this as her country but her colour seems to indicate to people that she is an 'OTHER' – from somewhere else.

My daughter calls me 'brown bread' mockingly when I recount meetings with predominantly white people, whom she calls 'white bread'. In the past, I would growl at her or mutter excuses, but now I realise that what she says is true. In this country, like many other Western countries, we need to look around and see all – the black, brown, multigrain people, the stripes and polka-dots that surround us. Why do I need to be defensive when I do not feel myself to be different? To tell you a secret: I have looked all people in the face and spoken my piece, because I have felt, deep inside me, that I am the same colour as the person I am talking to. Perhaps this unconscious belief has been grounded in my sense of equity.

At other times, she describes me as being a 'coconut', brown on the outside, white on the inside. I seem to be full of food analogies here; I am glad I am not a cream sponge cake or a beige-coloured meringue like some colleagues. Perhaps it is in keeping with their wimpy nature when it comes to taking a stand on racism and sexism. I like to say that my coconut-like personality is aptly described in an Indian proverb: 'The heart of an excellent person resembles a coconut – which though hard on the outside contains refreshing water and delicious food within.' All that said, I am proud that my skin *ain't* dirty but a beautiful tan brown.

This young woman, who has only known Australia as home, is regularly asked 'Where are you from?' which continues to puzzle and perplex her. It is the same question that has irritated me for years. You may ask why this question seems 'offensive' or 'exclusionary' to people from various ethnic backgrounds who may have lived in a western or developed country for one or more generations? My research shows that it is a fairly common question asked of people who don't have Anglo-Celtic looks in the UK, Europe, USA, Canada, and Australia. Jokes and experiences are seen on You-tube and other social media platforms on this issue. Because it implies 'You are not from around here' or 'You don't belong' or 'you are trying to define or label me' minutes after meeting me when you barely know me. And it often leads to more intrusive and insensitive questions which are not appropriate at any point unless the person being questioned chooses to share personal information willingly. Why do people need to be defined by their skin colour and facial features? Don't they have other traits, skills, intelligences, values, that make them intrinsically interesting to know?

I want to tell those who ask me or my daughter or other friends of colour the ethnic or colour question: "We are the citizens of this country, the same way you are. If you want to be friends, ask us the normal questions others ask when they first meet each other. Have you seen a good movie lately? What sort of music do you like? Have you got a great hobby?" We don't want to be your friends if you are simply collecting ethnic personalities to share with your friends and show them that you have these personal mascots or badges to wear on your sleeve to tell others what a great 'democratic' equaliser or bunny-hugger you are, what a wonderful friend to ethnic people. Don't let your social insensitivity in digging out people's ethnic origins and making them feel like some excluded or exotic species symbolise that you want them in your inner circle. We don't belong in some Hollywood movie where the wonderfully liberal and equalising parents discovered that pulling people of colour or race to your breast was a great social idea but one they could only admire and praise at a distance but not truly put into practice.

I have told so-called friends and adopted family members who say that it is interesting to find out people's origins and ethnicity that it makes me and my daughter and others like us feel 'other', bizarre, exotic or different. I have asked some: 'Would you ask a person in a wheelchair or a person with scarred facial skin: 'What happened to you?' 'No', they reply, 'that would be insensitive'. I appeal to them: 'Why not apply the same sensitivity to people from different ethnic backgrounds as you do to people who lack limbs or have facial scars'.

People still fail to understand that asking 'where are you from?' and doing so under the guise of curiosity or wanting to know a person's ethnicity is a hidden form of racism or indicative of unconscious bias. Perhaps, it is their way of putting me in my place, making me feel excluded from 'white' Australia and from the 'white' way of life. I believe I am being subtly told 'You are an OTHER' (perhaps Martian), definitely not one of us. Their words imply that I am not and can never be part of their cultural and social club.

When I try to explain how I feel on being asked such questions or directly challenge their motives, the racism turns to defensiveness, condescension or patronage. Coyly, they reply that it is nice to find out where people are from... but they refuse to accept that it is socially insensitive or invasive. Some white women insist that they want to know because it is interesting. In my more angry moments, I ask them: 'Tell me when you last had sex or stolen something from your boss'... I too would like to know!

I have also had the dubious and unhappy experience of being in a group where a person declares that he/she is the only Australian there, judging others in the room by their skin-colour or ethnicity. On one occasion I placed my hand on the person's shoulder and asked, 'And how old are you?' He said 'twenty-eight'. To which I replied that

I had been in Australia for almost forty years as an adult so I was more entitled to be called Australian than he was'. He did get the point. These days I say that the real Australians are the Indigenous people of this land. All the rest of us who have arrived – white or brown or other colours and ethnicities – are living here because of their grace and good will.

RACISM AND SEXISM IN POLITICS AND CORPORATE LIFE

I feel sad and almost ungrateful when I recount these experiences. There is no doubt that many people have treated me decently, as a regular human being. However, as marketing experts know, people remember their dreadful experiences at ten times the rate of good experiences. Recently, one of Australia's politicians made some 'whitesplaining' comments (defined by a news magazine as a white person complaining about diversity) saying he is offended that he is called a 'white male'. This sounds rich when the white, male bastion has been in power and laid down the rules and mores of society for hundreds of years. I wanted to say to him 'Don't feel sorry for yourself, mate. You have no idea how hard it is to be a brown, black or other coloured person or even a white woman in Australia. Nor do you know what it feels like to be an older person i.e. over fifty, whether you are white or a person of colour. I invite you to join the queue of those of us who have been offended and harassed because of various acts of racism and sexism including the use of numerous pejorative and patronising labels to describe women of colour . And I am sure you will agree that they are all undeserved.'

It seems that Australian boardrooms (like their counterparts in the UK, Europe, USA and Canada) are still predominantly 'male, pale and stale' as stated in a recent report published by an Australian university. Ninety percent of publicly-listed boards in Australia are filled by people from Anglo-Celtic backgrounds despite the fact that twenty –five percent of Australians are from non-European backgrounds. Such white, middle-aged males who sit at the top of the corporate tree make up less than seven percent of the total population. One board member said it was natural human instinct to associate with people that look and feel and speak like them. Males who served on boards say that in order to get somewhere, you need to keep your head down, speak with an Australian accent and belong to a matey club. Women from diverse backgrounds faced the highest barriers to entry. They experience double jeopardy through the combination of their gender and cultural background...as the supply of culturally diverse women is stunted at the executive level, making it difficult if not impossible to rise to the board level. In fact, one non-Anglo woman board member said she was 'tired of being asked for recipes from her homeland rather than being listened to by her colleagues and asked about her strategic insights'. I agree with her entirely.

This means that women of colour including myself have very little chance of getting in. Getting to executive level for me was a huge, upward battle for me. I was not white, nor blonde and did not have an Australian accent, though I had excellent degrees from Australian universities. White women have begun to make it to executive and board positions but they still remain in the minority – currently less than 30% of board positions are occupied by females and the same woman may hold a position on several boards. And when catastrophes happen or the institution they represent is in deep trouble, the chief executive or chair has to fall on her sword as seen in recent examples from the Banking Royal Commission. When a female chair or Chief Executive Officer is fired, the reports are sexist in nature because they contain not only the woman's name but her IQ, beauty regimen, the number of children she has and what has happened to her spouse, something that does not happen to the males who head corporations or chair various boards.

Another pompous and 'hollow' statement recounted to me by many recruiters, high-ranking corporate executives and board directors is that they promote on merit. The business of merit is a fallacy according to many women who know that it is a term which means standards and skills that are set by the men in power. When I read or hear that women are blamed for their lack of promotion opportunities, it tells me that there is an assumption of a level playing field for the country's top jobs. The majority of people don't seem to understand the concept of unconscious bias — the prejudices and the stereotypes we hold but are unaware of — which play a significant role in denying women a place at the core of public and private sector decision-making in Australia.

Perhaps I should not be so thin-skinned but I can't help it. It feels like people keep picking the scab on a sensitive wound until I flare up and snap at them. Inclusion, diversity, multi-culturalism – I have heard those words trotted out under all sorts of guises. I wonder if these concepts are skin deep; people talk about it but do not realise that their behaviours and words reveal hidden, unconscious racism. This, of course, does not beat the full-on, blatant racism –such as shouts of 'go on you black bitch', 'go back to where you came from'.

Being offended, harassed and humiliated is *de rigeur* for many women even today. The twenty-first century has not brought the depth and range of changes that many of us women had hoped it would. I had believed that things would be better for my daughter and her generation but it looks as if that is still a pipe dream. Women are still complaining of being discriminated against, of being put down, demeaned and their skills minimised.

LEAVING CORPORATE LIFE TO WORK AT MY PASSIONS

This brings me to the third whammy - that of ageism. It is an insidious form of discrimination not just against the elderly but against anyone somewhat older than us. These days it seems that anyone over forty-five or fifty dreads the age issue. A consulting firm recently reported that discrimination against older workers could well surpass sexism as one of the most important workplace issues today. It said that ageism was becoming the new sexism in the workplace as the population aged and economic pressures meant more people had to work later into their lives. I know that it affects people at both ends of the spectrum – the young who are trying to get into the workforce or start careers and the older worker – probably fifty plus years old – who is attempting to stay current and employable.

As I have grown older, I have had people of all ages disrespect and demean me – either unwittingly or consciously. Collecting wisdom, knowledge and experience via academia, corporate and personal life in this country for the majority of my adult years seems to bypass most people's consciousness. As I have grown older, I have had hints passed in my hearing of an 'old, ethnic woman'. I heard these terms so many times that I grew tired of the sexist innuendos, bullying and disparagement of my knowledge and skills; I realised there was a growing prejudice against older workers (ageism) and made the decision to leave corporate Australia.

I discovered that I no longer fitted into one of the three categories I had enjoyed: child, teenager, adult, middle-aged woman but was now classified as a senior citizen, elderly (!), old crone... or as some friends put it 'wrinkly, demented, pensioner'. This meant the time had come to reconsider my career and work options. I had been letting people know that while I may be categorised as a senior, I still had lots of quirky hobbies and pastimes, and I was just as lively, curious and adventurous as the cohorts of Gen X, Y and Z. I hadn't taken to motor-bikes and sky-diving yet but that could come. I was certainly not going to sit at home watching endless re-runs of TV shows and doing knitting.

I learnt 'new' technology and became fairly proficient with Facebook, Instagram, Twitter and other social media. I read a lot online, bought my products online from all over the world, downloaded my music, binge-watched Netflix and iView and had a number of apps for a variety of purposes. I went and still go to a gym twice a week with other seniors and have a watch which monitors my daily and weekly health and exercise. I began learning new languages and vocabularies besides German and French such as being YOLO (you only live once) and even contemplated getting a tattoo such as 'Carpe Diem' or 'You only live once'. I did not aim to nor will I sit and let the world pass me by.

My wits and cognition were still sharp, and my skills and insights into humans and their behaviour were getting even better. I believed I was morphing into a 'woman of wisdom'. So I decided to take time to recalibrate and enjoy my life doing the things that really interested me.

Entering retirement and leaving paid corporate work proved to be a blessing in disguise. It allowed my spirit and voice to float free. I no longer needed to worry about toeing the company line. I did not have to keep my feelings and opinions about what I was experiencing or observing under wraps. It seemed that a weight had lifted off me – the weight of being conscious of corporate politeness! I could stop worrying about combating racism, sexism and ageism, thumb my nose at misogyny, and permit myself to do the things that really mattered to me. My turn to live life to the full and tell my truth without fear or favour had come insidiously but not too soon.

BECOMING A SENIORPRENEUR - FORAY NO.1

Becoming a senior enabled me to enter another stage of life. Like the caterpillar, I was able shed the chrysalis of my old body parts and undergo a 'metamorphosis' emerging as a beautiful butterfly. Something changed within me. Life became exciting. The shackles seem to have dropped from my wrists and ankles, my soul felt lighter and I could feel a thrill in my heart. I didn't need to be a proper corporate woman. I felt I could let go of the restraints and really be me. I could reinvent myself. I examined all the business opportunities and social ventures I could possibly engage in.

First, I drew up a list of people who should be invited to my funeral, including what was to be worn, music to be played and all the other minute details of the celebratory after-party! I began composing my own eulogy as part of a 'roast' or a 'living funeral' so that I got to hear and enjoy what people would say about me. I even chose my coffin style – white chipboard – with several felt-pen markers where people could write about their experiences of me as a human being. This is not meant to be depressive or doleful but to embrace the transient nature of earthly life and its impermanence. The state of mind is called *Wabi Sabi* in Japanese: when translated it means to live in a way that finds beauty in the imperfections of this life and accepts the natural cycle of growth and decay.

I contemplated various post-retirement careers and opportunities: becoming a madam in a brothel - more on this later; selling cemetery plots on a party plan; designing and producing coffins with decoupaged photo-collages; designer of incontinence pads with photos of well-known public faces or nasty old relatives; denture designer with diamonds studded in teeth to show relatives where the wealth is hidden; running an elder cash converter social media page where 'oldies' sell pieces of the inheritance to their inheritors at 50% interest rather than the normal emotional blackmail; companion for singletons who want a Granny-Grandpa backpacker travel service; 'pet-napping' or 'pet-adopting' serving friends who have seen neighbours' pets neglected and abused or wish to make arrangements for their pets go to a happy foster home when they pass on.

I made a list of all the things I had never done before. I pierced my nose and added a tiny sparkling diamond to finish the look. I joined a gym to get fit and lose a few pounds, went on shopping forays for new and 'younger-looking' clothes and got a new smart phone. I even learnt the secrets of Tinder but none of the guys on the site excited me – perhaps I wanted an older and elegant Indiana Jones type but kept getting staid, corporate-type stuffed shirts whom I thought I had left behind. And I was still bored!

One of my impulsive sidelines in retirement work was to apply to become a personal assistant to a sex-worker. I emailed my corporate resume (as V.P. of HR) in reply to an advertisement in a local magazine. I thought this would allow the hiring person to see the breadth and scope of my skills but I think I was being lazy in not aligning my skills to the job requirements. Soon after emailing my resume, I was filled with horror at my impulsiveness closely followed by a thread of excitement. A little voice inside me said 'Hey what would Mum say, if she knew?'

Soon I had an email reply where the person asked to meet with me in a cafe after 6pm. In a dark and poorly lit corner sat a woman with a red wig, dark glasses and a bicycle helmet on the table sipping a lemon cough drink. She welcomed me cordially saying she had just come from 'work', cycling down the city streets to meet me and mentioned the name of a very well-known 'house of pleasure' to let me know that she was not an ordinary call girl.

She said she was amazed and curious to know why I wanted the job in view of my corporate career history. But she agreed to give me a trial saying she already had one good applicant who would do the basic administrative duties and she wanted someone else to develop the business that is applying for bank loans, contacting city councils and regulatory bodies to start a new 'service business' out of an apartment she intended to buy. She also wanted me to look after the financial, marketing and business issues of the new venture.

I threw myself into the business venture, researching various on-line marketing opportunities including social media and classy tabloids complete with photographs and explicit descriptions. I prepared plans, reports and spreadsheets to share with my new 'boss'. We met in dimly-lit cafes to discuss progress. She was very pleased with what I had done and added more detail to the documents I prepared. She paid me as per our verbal agreement and was warm and encouraging – very different to most of the people I had previously worked for in organisations.

We developed a friendly relationship. At one stage, she encouraged me to join her ranks! I was incredulous. I cried: 'Me? I am sixty-five, not very fit, and certainly too naive to know all the tricks and traps of your trade!' 'You don't need those', she said. 'Many of my clients only want to kiss and cuddle. I have colleagues in my workplace who are in their fifties and work alongside me - that is all they do and they make money'.

Three months later, it was time for a performance review. She was very encouraging and told me she was ready to promote me to the next step, with a small salary raise. I had never experienced her brand of kindness and positivity in my corporate role. Pleased with my performance she wanted to offer me the role of manager - of her website, business and the new salon she would open shortly. (I thought, I could have been a madam after being a corporate madam mediating some disgraceful behaviour!) I had found a good and caring boss, genuinely kind and generous but I was scared of the next step. My 'bucket list' now had one big tick against a long list of 'things I want to do and where want to go'. However, other places and opportunities beckoned. I resigned, got my final pay, had a farewell drink with my boss and went on my onward journey seeking zen and dedicating myself to the art of self-acceptance and maintenance.

BUSINESS SENIORPRENEUR – FORAY NO. 2

My next adventure into *seniorpreneurship* led me almost simultaneously into the world of small business and education. I have always loved jewellery – particularly coloured or semi-precious stones set in silver in what is known the new, art jewellery fashion. So I bought into a shop which retailed crystals, jewellery and new age books along with therapies such as massage, counselling and coaching. This fitted in with my intention to pursue a Masters degree in Applied Psychotherapy because I had decided that coaching and counselling were where my interests lay. I had also finished a teaching qualification the previous year which allowed me to enter the field of tertiary teaching. The new qualification was serendipitous. Over the course of the next four or five years, I taught at two TAFE (Technical and Further Education) colleges, a private college and two universities - in Sociology, Social Policy, Organisation Change and Development, Human Resources, Management, Procurement Policy, and Business Studies to name a few subjects. I enjoyed combining my life wisdom with my corporate knowledge and experience and academic disciplines to teach younger people and fuel their passion.

While I loved surrounding myself with jewellery and new age books, the routine of ordering, procurement and managing a shop which was open seven days a week soon ground me down. The creative part of the business turned out to take up ten percent of my time and the administrative, invoice-paying and sales parts of the business took up ninety percent of my time six days a week. Soon this became boring and tedious. So I sold my share in the jewellery and crystals venture after a couple of years and decided to concentrate on my Masters study in Psychotherapy, while expanding my private practice in counselling, coaching and teaching at tertiary level. Psychotherapy had drawn me from the mid-nineties when I fell into it by 'accident' believing it would enhance my Human Resources work. Within the first few months of my studies in counselling and psychotherapy, I discovered my personal *raison d'etre* and began to understand the whys and wherefores of my life experiences, behaviours and thinking. I began to understand the concepts of 'differentiation' and 'individuation' that is to discover my life's purpose, understand why I am the person I am today without the automatic hot-buttons, triggers and reactions which could be related to my socialisation and early experiences.

I finished my Masters' studies in Psychotherapy concentrating on psychodynamics, somatic therapy and narrative therapy. These are useful modalities in my practice as a counsellor and executive coach because they are congruent with my stand as a compassionate and non-judgemental person. I use a humanistic, person-centred approach to help people explore their own journey of personal development and the potential that exists in them; such work also allows them to work with issues such as relationship matters or life events and changes such as loss and grief caused by death, divorce or 'empty-nest' feelings. When this is combined with psychodynamic work such as exploring one's past including difficulties and trauma in early childhood, teenage and adult years, it helps clients to understand what has led them to make certain choices as adults or act out various behaviours. The addition of somatic therapy allows people to understand and incorporate the genesis or existence of bodily experiences such as anxiety, churning in the gut, headaches, back-aches and the inter-relationship of these physical phenomena with psychological experiences. This is based on a solid understanding based on evidence-based study and practice in the field that thought, emotion and bodily experiences are all inextricably linked. A change or healing in one domain can affect and flow on to other areas of the body and psyche. This understanding and insight has helped my coaching and therapy practice to grow as it is grounded in academic learning as well as my own personal experience plus those of my clients.

My academic studies, teaching and private practice in counselling, coaching and consulting fed my inner person, my psyche.

However, part of me missed the hustle-and-bustle of corporate life and business entrepreneurship which is the public and external part of being in the world. Finding an opportunity to practice my jewellery-making skills, I came across another business for sale - a Jewellery training school - which I ran for a few years. Again the routine of administration, procurement, and responsibility for everything from insurance to marketing, palled on me. Design and creativity only formed a small percentage of my work week and the rest was routine. I also learnt a lot of lessons along the way in honesty and trust. At times, my values of kindness were exploited by some to take advantage of me. This time my life lessons were focused on learning to hold my boundaries and voice my concerns in a positive, non-aggressive way. My wake-up call came when my favourite nephew died suddenly in an accident and I had to find friends and locum managers to run the business while I went to assist and support my grieving sister. I also needed to take time out to get over my own loss and sadness. This led me to sell the business and give myself time to recover. My nephew's death, followed shortly after by the deaths of two close friends, led me to consider my own mortality.

I resolved to engage in work and activity that gave me joy and fed into my passions.

This time I was firmly back on the road to academia, coaching and writing and my personal journey would be reflected in the work I did. I began teaching counselling and sociology subjects at an institution for applied psychology and therapy. At the same time, my coaching and counselling practice began to grow. I expanded my consulting work into leadership coaching, managing organisation change, facilitating conferences in diversity and inclusion and leading cross-cultural seminars. I was invited to speak on issues of sexual harassment in the workplace by women's groups who had been in the media and later by people who ran companies which put films on our screens (just after #MeToo). Now I get regular invitations to participate in events and panels discussing women's rights including pay equity, right to a harassment-free workplace, support and coaching required by women in small and medium – sized businesses, addressing the needs of women from culturally and linguistically diverse backgrounds and programs to empower women to understand their legal, political and social rights.

Friends congratulate me on occasion and at other times pity me. Some tell me to stop racing around and learn to be sedate and spend time reading, working in the garden, watching a little television and travelling to spend my savings. I love the latter. Travel to distant lands appeals to me. I am glad I have travelled all through my 'gypsy' life – it almost seems that every two and a bit years I feel the travel bug bite and decide to go wandering. There are so many places on my bucket list. My wandering is soul-satisfying because not all who wander are lost. I have a map pinned to the wall in my hallway – two maps in fact. One map shows push pins of cities and countries where I have wandered and the other shows large push pins of places I still have to visit. The race is on – to see the most places before I spend my savings or my knees and hips give out.

My love of travel has also been a source of renewal. Travel runs deep in my family's genes and psyche. My grandparents visited Europe in the mid-1930s, travelling to the UK, France, Switzerland and Italy and also visiting Germany where the publicity machine of the Third Reich was doing a lot of spin-doctoring. They came to regret that particular visit because they felt they had been duped but they continued to travel to areas of the world to see places and people for themselves. (Read the stories of my grandparents later in this book.) My parents and three siblings have followed in this tradition and we keep journals, logs and maps of the places we have visited. The next generation consisting of my daughter, nephews and nieces have also taken up this tradition. We compare notes on places and monuments not money and real-estate. We also have one trait in common – we never bring back many photographs, if any. Travel feeds our souls and the pictures live in our memories.

These days I have another reason for travelling - different yet very suitable to travelling to distant lands. Three years ago, my sister lost her only child in a motor-cycle accident and has grieved for him deeply. He was like a son to me and I have wept many tears for him. He was a lively, intelligent young man who loved to explore new things, all things comic and extraordinary. We had a beautiful friendship and a lot of things in common. Travel and adventure were a common, almost genetic trait; a few times we met overseas - miles from home - and enjoyed a few days of seeing new sights and enjoying novel adventures. Six months after he died, I suggested to my sister that we meet in England and travel to a few places in northern Europe that her son had been to. She took up the offer and it gave her comfort - one to visit the places her son had been to and deeply enjoyed; two - that she would go with me and I would give her the space and time to talk about him and their life together before he died. She told me that this form of grief support-cum-travel therapy helped her tremendously and it helped me too on my journey of grief and loss. Last year, we went to eastern Europe to visit museums, monuments and enjoy the magical scenery. We had exciting adventures on buses and trains and made our way to Turkey to see beautiful historical monuments from the Byzantine era in Istanbul and Izmir, the site of ancient Ephesus. Her deep love for her son and doing things that he loved are incorporated into our travels and she feels that he is present, laughing and clowning and striding along with us as we visit different places.

Getting older has brought time for reflection and understanding – both for myself and others. Like many of my clients, I have wanted to and continue to make sense of my life. I remember a client I saw - who said his reason for coming to therapy was because he wanted to get 'the knots out of his hair'. He wanted to understand the course of his life and make his path smoother as he went forward. That statement encapsulates why therapy is important – besides restoring us to mental and emotional wellness, it helps us to understand why and what we have done may have contributed to the so-called problems in life. This has mirrored my own journey in the therapy room, in coaching clients and working for a better world for women. I have come to understand that my own behaviours and actions were not just mindless and fruitless acts but outcomes and end points of journeys which started thirty, forty or more years ago. Hence I have felt the need to recount my story in this book to understand and connect my early life, adult and middle-age experiences to the way I feel and the activities I engage in today. I am still working out why I cry or don't cry when things happen. I have come to understand why I have strong philosophical views on a lot of subjects including my 'rampant' feminism. That it has come as a result of violence and abuse and having had no control of my life as a matured. My feminism has also come alive from being disrespected by men and patriarchal religions who said 'Trust me, would I lie to you?' as they steamrollered me by demeaning and controlling me.

THERAPIST AND COACH – SENIORPRENEUR FORAY NO. 3

The transition which has brought me into the 'third age' of my life has been steady but transformational. I have enjoyed moving into a time where I have become the wise crone, the guide, a coach, teacher and mentor to others. My relationships have transmogrified themselves along the way. I have learnt that life has been leading me in a certain direction over the past many years. And I have accepted it – gladly! On reflecting on my turn of career and work, I have realised both the personal circumstances, the skills and attitude which have pointed me in this direction and the experiences (good and bad) along the way have made me who I am. It has helped to 'grow' ME.

I have come to enjoy speaking and presenting ideas particularly on issues which feed my passion. Public speaking has been normal for me for most of my life from ten years of age when my mother encouraged us to engage in door-to-door proselytising to college days when I engaged in debates to speaking in my corporate and post-retirement careers such as coaching and education. I have become better at it and more successful as I have matured. Speaking has such high impact - I have loved connecting with people, getting up in front of them (despite my initial bout of nervousness) and reaching out to them with ideas and inviting a call to action. I have worked at and become better in the dark arts of writing. I am told that one of the ways we market ourselves is via - writing and speaking and I have loved speaking, writing and 'selling ideas' from my teens onwards. I have been able to speak on a variety of subjects with confidence and pride. These days I focus on the things that delight me – social justice issues particularly to do with women's economic, political, social and personal power. Marketing and selling ideas is fun - it is not a chore or a burden because I am sharing powerful words with people – something that is giving them knowledge and skills. I have worked to get into roles which allow me to be the 'point person' and have enjoyed it. It has gone from being a necessary evil to being something that is fun and rewarding, I focus on building my coaching, educating and mentoring relationships so that they are there for the long term. I am serious about getting them to understand what they have to do (just as I did) to be better people, managers, partners, workers.

Like my friends and clients, I want to know about the next thing on the horizon, what I need to be prepared for and how I can then help and interact with people to help them break through to their next level of growth. I see education (formal and academic) whether it be personal, therapeutic or developmental as an investment and time spent in it brings a big return on investment. We don't need to know exactly what is important at any given point of time. When we identify a gap, we need to fill it because all education and development is a valuable investment. On the way, we learn what is critical and that is a feedback loop which leads to a love of learning that will last a lifetime.

I believe that knowledge is not just a piece of data, sterile and immobile. It is something we need to transfer to another who does not possess it so that their lives and psyches can be affected and changed. I also believe that all learning is relational and knowledge is produced through interaction. When I interact as a coach and educator, I believe I am giving value by being actively engaged in a learning dialogue which makes a difference to my own and my clients' lives.

Semi-retirement which allowed me to go into coaching, counselling and writing has also provided me with a lot of reading time. I read everything from labels on jam jars to crime fiction to memoirs to travel books and advances in therapeutic techniques. My commitment to self-development has me attending workshops and classes in everything from 'Being a Social Activist in Women's Affairs' to 'Dealing with complicated Trauma' to 'Why our country needs a Bill of Rights'. I believe I am more open-minded and progressive in my views than many a person hailing from the Millenial or Gen X or Y generations. While it has come later in life, I want people to know what it means to be discriminated against, stared at because of your avant-garde views, help people to become conscious of their 'unconscious bias' if any and to help women and girls on their journey to being equal and free from harassment.

During my business ownership years I joined an international women's business organisation for networking, support and marketing purposes. Two years ago, I was elected state chief of one of these organisations which enabled me to step up into a role which supported women in business and enabled them to have their voices heard at government and senior corporate levels, discuss the barriers they faced to becoming larger businesses and getting support and advice from the business network. While women are the major contributors and starters of small business, their access to banking, financial and government assistance remains at low levels. Once again, I was able to engage in having our voices heard and our problems and needs understood – again from the perspective of personal experience.

Hearing the news on community radio led me to volunteer at the same radio station. Now I use my voice to reach an audience which may be visually limited or unable to access print. I read the news from national daily newspapers once a week and also read articles from known weekly socio-political magazines. This has led to reading books I have personally enjoyed for broadcast to listeners. I feel honoured that my love of the English language and the written word is finally being recognised. I smile as my unconscious has led me to find joy in using my voice to serve others in this way.

In terms of religion, I have finally come to a place of peace within myself. There are times, I believe my heart is closed to the traditional religious lessons that were inculcated in me; however, at the right time I will come to know what to believe and how to go forward. I don't describe myself as agnostic or atheist or a follower of some mysticism currently revealed or about to take place. In the meantime, I believe I am a spiritual person, one who loves and is part of a larger environment of living beings and the universe. I don't feel greater than or lesser than anyone – human, animal, plant, mineral or other. Humility, observing and really listening with an open heart, examining all sides of every story, and showing compassion and empathy stay with me. I resonate with the words: I am a spiritual being having a human experience.

The invisibility that I had feared as I approached my senior years no longer concerns me. Being engaged in a variety of activities that interest me at a mental and soul level has kept me going. The same activities have allowed me to contribute as a mature human being. Recently I heard someone say that social activism was a form of therapy! It sure is.

FEMINISM — MY WAY

My growing passion for women's rights and women's legal, social and political empowerment has led me to join certain women's organisations to advocate for women's rights, raise awareness to stop domestic violence, support local women's refuges and fund education and empowerment of girls in under-developed countries, support young women in high school to take their stand in public policy and business, and women's pay equity among many other relevant women's issues.

Another organisation I work with also works in the same field locally: it helps educate and empower women about their political, legal and personal rights including reproductive rights,, end violence against women and stamp out sexual harassment in the workplace among various campaigns. I also volunteer with a crisis support agency for women from south-east Asia, particularly those who have come as refugees or dependants or professional visa holders. The rate of domestic violence in communities which have gone through migration trauma or where rigid patriarchal control is accepted is very high and resources are very low. Two issues that concern me deeply at the moment and which loom large under the surface of placid seas like an iceberg are dowry abuse and forced marriage. The tales of women with this narrative break my heart and call for action and support.

The theme of social justice particularly for women's rights continues to inspire me - in my reading, writing and activism – using my voice, insights, skills and experiences. I am able to talk about issues we face with honesty and passion, to appeal to people's consciences and advocate another and better way of participating in community life. My work has encompassed working with women undergoing domestic violence; educating women in their civic rights; coaching women to succeed in business or academia or in not-for-profit company roles. And now I use my voice and enthusiasm to help women from Indigenous and multi-cultural backgrounds to get their just and deserved rights and work their way to the front of the line!

However, my thinking and philosophy regarding women's rights to homes, communities and workplaces free of sexism and racism has turned away from what my daughter calls the' middle-aged white women's brand of feminism'. She has witnessed my conversion to feminism for over thirty years and would initially taunt me for being like 'white feminists'. This is indeed true as I read and research my topics; I find that the papers are written from a white woman's perspective and wants e.g. 'my husband and I fight over what to get as new furniture' or 'how does a woman deal with an elder- or grandchildren care when her own family is grown up?' I feel like yelling Hooray. Do you know how multi-cultural women have dealt with child care when their children were little? As one Turkish woman told me: 'We used to tie our children by a long twist of cloth to the dining table and go out to work, asking grandma or the woman next door to keep an eye on the children.' Other multi-cultural women have not argued with their husbands regarding what to get in terms of new furniture or who to marry their daughters to – that was decided by the patriarchs in the family! Know this: problems of the developed world are vastly different to the problems of the developing (third) world'.

INTERSECTIONAL FEMINISM

My philosophy regarding feminism is simple: it is the right of every woman to have equality and individuality as humans and be accepted as such by her community and society. Every woman needs to have her experiences accepted as genuine and her feelings and beliefs are an integral part of her desire to be equal and free. Whether she has faced control and domination from men (patriarchy at large or the men in her life – father, brothers, husband, sons) including being the subject of family violence or has been demeaned and held back because of the structures and systems based on race, gender, age, sexuality, ethnicity, culture, ability, social status or any other device constructed by the power-holding classes in society. Each of these segregating structures intersect at various points with others and so many women undergo the compounding fractures and burdens imposed by these artificial divisions and –isms. This I understand is called **intersectional feminism.** It took me so long to understand and accept the meaning of this term. I understood this only when I realised that the 'white-brand' of feminism had failed to answer my queries and provide me with the answers to dismantle these structures.

I have talked to many women, mostly white women, some of whom claim to be feminists but others who think of it as a dirty word. Many of the women I have talked to accept that our differences are individual and unique but here we come to a parting of ways. Those who think feminism is a dirty word want us to continue as if nothing has happened and slowly and inevitably the world will change for the better. Wrong! I have been waiting for that for the past forty years and to hear it said now by conservative mostly white women makes me angry. Such white women and men shut their ears and thinking to the need for quotas and targets. And the white feminists who think if we play in the middle ground of feminist politics for the sake of solidarity believe we will all get carried along on a gentle or perhaps massive wave of change and get to a place of equality. Both groups of women (and I am leaving men who are either under the hypnotic influence of patriarchy or marginally out of its range) fail to understand the politics and mind-set of 'white privilege'. Yes, they are aware of the existence of the glass ceiling and glass walls but their strategies seem either one-size fits all and strident or subtle. What bugs me is that they deny the existence of white privilege and the advantages it affords them nor do they accept that the struggle for women of colour, age, ability, ethnicity and other intersections is both difficult and different.

Intersectionality by definition refers to the inter-relationship of cultural patterns of oppression. Such oppression is closely interwoven and influenced by the embedded systems of society which include race, gender, class, ability, and ethnicity.

Intersectionality is a concept that should unite us because we (as women) have fundamentally common experiences of disadvantage and similar goals for equality. So many women in this world have multiple layers of so-called disadvantage in their lives that they have to deal with. Hence, the 'one-size-fits-all' type of feminism is not going to work! The feminist movement which was started by mainly white, middle class, cis-gendered and able-bodied American and European women in the 1960s and 1970s, whilst admirable in getting the subject into people's consciousness, cannot fill the current space for women from around the world who are oppressed or disadvantaged by a multiplicity of so-called disadvantages e.g.

colour, ethnicity, disability. For example, I am an older woman with brown skin from the Indian sub-continent and I have encountered domestic abuse, religious control by patriarchal religion and also bear the scars of racism, sexism and ageism as I navigate life, work and the society.

The affluent western country I live in gave me the courage and impetus to be myself. I was able to break the shackles of controlling men and patriarchal religion and fight for my rights, leaping over a number of obstacles at every turn. I left my 'home land', then a situation of domestic violence, learnt new skills, educated myself to a significant tertiary level, became a single parent and underwent much adversity, and finally learnt to speak up against racism and sexism and now ageism. I also found friends and supporters in this distant land, a place which I had never envisaged living in when I was growing up, who have shown genuine care and friendship for me, helping me in a dozen ways, people who have made me come to terms with the deep inner strengths I possess and to act and speak with courage and dignity. Perhaps the act of coming to another land was courageous in itself, though daunting. I have slowly absorbed consciously and unconsciously the culture of being an individual and acting from my core inner values and beliefs. It has been a long journey, emotionally, politically, socially, culturally.

I heard, with great pride, my daughter describe me to a group of people by saying – 'my mother is a self-made woman'. She went on to recount experiences of our poverty when we first set up home when she was five years old – living in two rooms, sharing with another family; often having to walk instead of using a bus when we had two dollars left at the end of the week; not having a car, then getting an old jalopy; how I had never depended on a husband for help; and finally becoming a successful corporate business woman.

All true. As a result of the obstacles and mountains, I have become ME, a woman of resilience and strength albeit stoic at times (but that is a result of my past experiences) as well as someone who has come into the twenty-first century experiencing and living a resolute and authentic inner and outer life.

THE REAL ME TODAY

An Indian mystic is reported to have said that we are responsible for what we are and whatever we wish ourselves to be. We have the power to make ourselves.

Reflecting on the effects of my heritage and upbringing, then the terrible experiences of domestic violence, sexism, racism and ageism, I wonder how it has shaped my life direction and my personality. How have I incorporated my values and interests and internalised the experiences from people who have affected me for better or worse? There are contradictions within me that colour my heart and soul.

The perspectives derived from my rootstock have sent deep striations through my new and adopted psyche. I am a graft on my adopted new tree of Australia because my soul brings its own meanings from the land of my birth and my upbringing. The stain of this upbringing is so deep that no matter how hard I try to be a citizen of this new and cherished land, my soul is sometimes caught in its past.

When confronted by these contradictions, my whole persona and psyche is challenged and wants to fight back. I believe I am not a foreigner in this or any other land but a unique citizen of the world because the values I had as a child and those that I have adopted in my adult years have added more layers of complexity and meaning. There is a part of me that needs to talk about it, to cleanse and re-program myself. I refuse to be seen as lonely, rootless, rejected, 'another' in an alien society. I want to be valued for myself and be an integral part of a just and caring society.

I believe my parents, grandparents, folk heroes and the cultural accoutrements with which I grew up had a profound effect on my life. My genetic make-up, my culture and traditions, then my philosophy of life and the variety of experiences as I grew into a young and then older woman have certainly contributed to who I am today. Every day I reflect on the things I do, the thoughts I have and the emotions I feel and compare them to what it was like growing up. And I am constantly amazed that I am such a different person today to what I was as a child or teenager or even a young woman.

I know I am not an automatic product of my biology, socialisation, education or life experiences. Nor can I lay claim to some great happenstance or a wonderfully happy childhood. (Never believe the latter when you hear it from family or friends; no one ever had a fabulously happy childhood unless they were living in La-La-Land.) Your antennae ought to go up if you hear that from anyone because everyone of us has had some dysfunctionality in our lives – growing up or experienced in our grown up lives. It's just that we may not have perceived it for what it was, are unconscious of it or we live in denial. The latter is more likely.

Saying all the above, you may think I am an egoist "a self-centred or selfish person" or even an egotist "an arrogantly conceited person". I claim to be intelligent; I love gathering information on a wide variety of subjects with my main interests being politics, history, art, literature, psychology and social relations. I was also taught never to be conceited by my grandparents and parents and saw that in action in their lives. Modesty and humility were key attributes according to these wise people – others had to see your wit and achievements and acknowledge them. But that has also been my downfall over the years in this foreign land. It has led arrogant or ignorant people to think I know nothing or need to be taught the basics; they start their patronising behaviour as if I were a little child or that little dark-skinned woman standing outside her hut waiting for the big white master or mistress to come around and teach me how to bow and curtsey or add two plus two!

When I put together my qualities of kindness and a certain, innate modesty, I have found it becomes a double-edged sword! People judge you on your dark skin and try to patronise you or pull 'fast ones' over you i.e. make jokes at your expense, thinking you haven't got the hidden meaning because you are too dumb to perceive it. That is the quality in myself that I both like and dislike because it often leads me to become a simmering pot of anger. I get cranky when patronised or dismissed because of my skin colour or race or age particularly when the person has not seen the whole me. I am also quite obsessive about certain things, mostly the slights and put-downs by people too naive to know better. I also obsess about what I have accomplished in life, believing there is very little time left to achieve what I want to.

My greatest growth over the last twenty years is knowing that I have found my voice and learnt to speak my truth. I have discovered that suppressing my sharp mind as a child and as a young woman due to societal and religious control left me with scars and internal burdens. For years, I had become too much of a people pleaser and did not do enough to grow my own self-approval and self-esteem. I am done with that. I refuse to be put down, exploited, derided whether gently or harshly or ridiculed.

Writing about the past has given me a lot of time to reflect on what I have learned in life. I am conscious of who I am, where I am going and the purpose of my life. At times, I have been afraid of falling and disappearing into a pit of loneliness, disappointment, abandonment and an overwhelming nostalgia. Add to this my horror of becoming an invisible older woman. There are times I have felt I am standing on a cliff-top, having lost my way to connect with a forgotten past and shaky in finding a way forward to a glowing future. Despite these inner feelings, I believe my life teeters between coming awake slowly and while at other times I have had 'meaning' hurled at me from a great height.

In the mean time, my soul and psyche are transforming in a magical and mystical manner. I understand 'awakening' is a process that can happen in this lifetime or perhaps over many different lifetimes. My learning and research tell me that awakening may happen as a 'family' process over many generations. Losses, sadness, resolutions of issues such as slavery, abandonment, searching for meaning and truth can take many generations. My studies in family therapy introduced me to a thereapeutic process which may aid in healing or resolving personal issues that may be generational in origin. Strangely, the Hindu belief of reincarnation of souls touches on this subject. And science is making discoveries in the process called epigenetics. The latter implies that features which are additional to the traditional genetic basis for inheritance such as chronic exposure to stress hormones in our bodies can cause changes or modifications to the DNA in the brains of mice and other animals.

Over the past few years, we have come to understand that trauma can transcend generations. This is seen in the effects recorded in current generations of Aboriginal people in Australia as a result of the 'stolen generations' saga where Indigenous children were taken from their parents and put into missions and homes never knowing their parents or their heritage. Various government reports give authoritative accounts and experiences of how it has affected the descendants of people who were 'stolen'. I have come to realise that this was the trauma and sadness suffered by my grandmother when she was taken from her family in the name of religion. It affected my mother and I feel the strains of sadness in my own psyche. Hence my allusions to the inheritance of values, interests, emotions, skills, longings from past members of my family as well as great people from the past, historical or familial, who have inspired or touched me.

A PERSONAL AWAKENING

The process of awakening that I have experienced has been on two levels. We can **grow through pain** *(*the Japanese word for this process is *Kensho)* or through **insight** (the Japanese word for the process is *Satori). Kensho* is a gradual process by which we come awake through many painful experiences. These experiences allow us to reflect and we gather insights incrementally allowing us to evolve spiritually, perhaps taking us to a state of enlightenment. It is similar to a marathon where we learn from mistakes, sufferings and pain, thus becoming better than before. The process of *kensho* does not guarantee freedom from pain or a state of enlightenment forever, just glimpses and awareness of future possibilities.

On the other hand, *Satori* is a form of sudden awakening when we become aware of the 'truth' and see things as they are without any filtering of information. It may be that 'aha' or 'light bulb' moment, sometimes painful but profoundly liberating. It could be awakening to a truth about ourselves or some aspect of the eternal truths of the universe. An example is making mistakes by entering a number of 'wrong' relationships or business ventures, which almost always fail and then discovering one day as we reflect that there was a painful pattern in what we had thought, done or said. Hence, it is growing up through a sudden and painful insight.

The process mentioned above has also been described as **transformation** which happens in two ways: one through a gradual accumulation of evolving meaning which happens over time. This means getting wiser as you grow older i.e. if you are reflective and open to it. That is slow growth. It cannot be forced or happen fast i.e. overnight. It is subtle and often undetected and it may happen in fits and starts. The other way to transformation or awakening is facing a sudden dilemma which disorients you and causes a lot of pain such as the ending of a relationship or losing your job or business or having to choose between two conflicting values.

The memories, experiences and learnings from my past have meant moments of great pain as seen in the process of *Satori*. The patterns I have seen in failed relationships, bouts of domestic violence, incidents of discrimination or rejection, going down the path of religion and then turning to a different spirituality have given me huge insights. And some incidents and experiences have been at a more mellow and subtle level. One of these learnings has been to discover that my kindness has been used by some to manipulate me into doing what they wanted me to do e.g. give them money. This learning has led me to improve my 'boundaries', discover the art of 'I' language and gently help others to respect me and what I will do and won't do. As I have discovered my patterns and failings, I have also felt an uprising of courage. My compassion and tolerance have grown deeper, my drive for justice stronger. I have learned to be a better person in many ways and a tougher person in other ways.

One of my greatest awakenings has been that I have survived and thrived after living through violence and abuse then discrimination coming from sexism, racism, injustice, harassment. I have experienced many ways that have sought to diminish me and my humanity. I have been humiliated and trodden on but I feel triumphant. When I hear people refer to me to as that 'little Indian woman', I am appalled at the manner with which I am dismissed and minimised. They do not see me as the spirited, intelligent woman who overcame so many obstacles and setbacks as a migrant, who made good and now works to give back to society so that all of us can have better lives.

I have had a relentless struggle for years – to bury the past and the painful memories it evokes or use my voice and skills to move towards getting equity and justice for myself and women like me. It has been a balancing act: I have mostly resolved the pain and heartache of domestic violence and religious control and believe I have left it behind. The experiences of racism and sexism however rankle within me particularly when I stumble over them again and again.

The saying to be the change we want to see in the world is a guiding light to me. According to the teachings of this great leader, we can make a difference and in fact it is our moral duty to do so. Like him I believe that the ends do not justify the means. In fact, we have to find new ways to bring about social and political change. We need to fight injustice with justice, violence with non-violence and oppression by embracing the oppressed and working for and with them. This is my road-map going forward – build bridges, bring racism and sexism to light but do so with honesty and compassion.

WISHES FOR THE FUTURE

I am comfortable with my life, my current work and the moral compass that guides me in my endeavours. I support women and children undergoing domestic violence to be safe and I want stricter laws and greater resources for women and children to be safe; I want access and funds allocated for maternal physical and mental health as well as lifelong psychological and mental health for women. I want greater resources for people in distress like refugees and homeless people because I too was a refugee from a home of violence, pushed out into what seemed an uncaring world, not knowing where to turn in a new country. I want equality and justice in any sphere where people are denied their human rights such as equal representation for women and migrants in political life. It took me much heartache and struggle to find my voice and I want other women to find their voices and be heard and their rights recognised in their fight for equality.

The principle of *Maya* (a Sanskrit/Hindi word) meaning compassion and benevolent love lives in my heart. It resonates with values of my parents and grandparents and the way they acted because of their compassion and care for those who had little. Those memories remain deep within me. Combined with my personal experiences and values, they have led me to work for women's empowerment – economically, politically, socially, legally. This has also led to my work in fighting for equal opportunity to women to work and progress in every sphere of activity they enter, thus breaking down glass walls, glass ceilings, glass floors. I also want equal pay for women because

I too had an enormous struggle to educate myself and progress in a career.

I have found fulfilment and happiness in helping women to get political, social, familial, legal or career equity; helping migrant men and women or those less familiar with the corporate climate get a job and a foot on the career ladder; finding accommodation and support for homeless men and women; pushing for women business entrepreneurs to market themselves and get access to grants and economic resources; listening to and assisting both men and women who have suffered domestic abuse; and supporting Indigenous First Peoples to claim their voice and opportunities. Because in the end I believe I am helping me.

If this is the way to redemption or *Nirvana,* so be it. I believe I am repaying the kindness and help given to me by friends and strangers who helped me or thinking of lessons learned the hard way. One of these was a Christian lay preacher whom I talked to forty years ago when I was destitute and depressed. He heard my sadness and pain and said to me, with some exasperation: 'You can keep crying for yourself and become bitter and twisted, or you can move on, learn from this and give back'. I have consciously learned the value of giving back or as some say 'pay it forward'. In fact, that has become my *mantra* for those undergoing similar pain and hardship, whether this be a career, relationship, domestic or personal failure – providing a listening ear, a compassionate heart and providing practical help and direction.

I am not personally destroyed by my experiences of domestic violence, sexism, racism or ageism. It is the reason I have chosen to speak about these so-called forbidden topics – the elephant in the room. While I have navigated the deep seas of misogyny and racism and sexism, I have managed to shrug off the experiences. I have become stronger and confident in my right to live, work and exist side by side with people of every colour, ethnicity, religion, race and gender. I have grown as a human being; I now take pride in being a feminist and activist and an outspoken advocate of women's rights in my adopted country. I have found my passion. For women to be safe and have the right to own and work for their economic security through equal pay, better superannuation, access to affordable housing, and have full rights to their bodies, intellects and power to make choices.

I came to this 'free' western world and discovered freedom and independence. My freedom or the awakening to the real me started at thirty. At thirty, I became a full-time working mother and soon after started post-graduate studies in Human Resources. At forty, I undertook a Masters degree in Commerce; at fifty, I changed education tracks and started studying psychotherapy at post-graduate level; at sixty-plus, I received a Masters degree in Psychotherapy and Counselling. I have followed my dreams, wherever they took me. I have tried new jobs, education, careers and life opportunities. It has been exhilarating and exciting.

My awakening as a feminist, a woman of wisdom and activism, started a few years after I arrived in Australia as a heart-broken and despairing woman. Within five years I had started on my upward trajectory in corporate and personal life. I remember travelling to Parliament House, Canberra, twice in the early nineteen nineties – once to receive an Award for my company's work in the Disability field and another time to take part in a consultation with the sitting government on women's needs and expectations. I remember seeing the magnificent tapestry in the Great Hall (based on a painting by Arthur Boyd) which seemed to be a painting of a forest though the weavers had sought permission from the artist to put in a glimpse of Halley's Comet into the tapestry. It brought back memories of the tears shed by my grandmother as she drew her recollection of Halley's Comet for me. I also remembered holding my grandfather's hand as a little girl and staring at the skies to see if I could get a glimpse of another magical comet or a shooting star. The tapestry in the Great Hall moved me to tears and caused me to reflect on how far I had come. I have found personal fulfilment and contentment along with material prosperity – all to a degree I had not dreamed of.

I had left my past behind (or the painful parts of the past) and discovered the values and issues that matter to me. I have been regenerated and found my *zen* and enthusiasm for life. I have gained the freedom to think independently without being influenced by previous religious and traditional beliefs and this helps make my personal journey a meaningful one. I am becoming more 'learned' in the true sense of the word and waking to my destiny at many levels – spiritual, emotional, social and psychological. I had found peace and discovered life is well worth living. I was also finding my passion and engaging in the issues that really matter.

My hope is now for my daughter, my nieces and nephews and their children and the ones who come after them to look up at the stars either when some old or new comet streaks through the sky and reflect that the world is indeed equal and just to people of all races, genders, political persuasions, ethnicities, social classes and occupations. The deep seas that have divided us as humans are indeed narrow and eminently navigable.

In the meantime, I continue to live my life as I always have: one foot in front of the other, face to the wind, marching on regardless. I am determined to live my life with freedom and ease, being colourful and honest and following my dreams.

THOUGHTS ON OVERT AND COVERT DISCRIMINATION (RACE, GENDER AND AGE)

I believe most overt discrimination has gone underground. A lot of systemic discrimination has been rooted out but covert pockets of discrimination remain because some people have stayed insular in their beliefs. Some of these people may be xenophobic. Some of the xenophobia and resultant discrimination, can pop out here and there like little boils, which if not checked, can grow larger and become malignant. Many people don't think first and then act; they let their curiosity sometimes combined with a lack of sensitivity take over, when crossing paths with someone new i.e. new because of their presumable ethnic background or colour. Sometimes they show their discomfort or curiosity with strange black, brown, and other coloured faces by asking 'Where are you from?' The question seems to be put in such a way as to put you in a box and label you. The person of different ethnicity or colour feels as if they may as well be an animal at the zoo with a plastic card on their cage giving a description of their genus, habitat and feeding habits. And once their curiosity is sated, they seem to want to patronise you without getting to know you as a whole person.

The curiosity based on a person's ethnic origin and the stereotyping that then follows continues into the modern day. A couple of years ago, one of Australia's leading daily newspapers reported on a photographic exhibition of a number of women from many ethnic backgrounds who have repeatedly been asked that question. A documentary series was also made for Australian television with a similar title, showing the superficiality of ordinary people's views - skin colour and ethnicity seem to be their star features! Not the person's intellect, personal life philosophy or history, knowledge, education, skills, hobbies or achievements!

The question 'Where are you from' that both puzzles and annoys me is not limited to Australia. Some Youtube videos on this topic are well worth watching as are TV documentaries on the same subject. A comedian whose family migrated from China over a hundred years ago says he gets asked this trite question 'Where are you really from?' – all the time. His experience is pretty common. No matter how long your family has been here, if you look a bit different either due to skin colour or facial features, the chances are you will get asked that question every other week. And each and every questioner is blissfully unaware that you have been asked the same thing and fobbed off people with the same answer a thousand times!

There is no doubt that we are more socially aware in our views (or should I say politically correct) than we were fifty years ago. Then the ruling class had the upper hand and categorised people through the lens of their stereotypical or discriminatory views. Racism was a result of economic and political domination in the 'new' worlds or colonies. The need for labour led to the practice of slavery closely attended by views that black people were inferior to white people with various forms of pseudo-scientific proof. Similarly, countries and their people that were being colonised for their economic resources found themselves divided into white European people who formed the ruling class and people of colour who were considered to be inferior and made into the working classes. However, de-colonisation found vast numbers of people of all colours and ethnicities dispersing and settling in all parts of the world. The new world and new century has meant appealing to and respecting a wide variety of people in a way that respects their individual dignity and worth.

I am acutely aware that people of all races practice various form of discrimination not only with people of their own race but also in dealing with people of other colours, ethnicities, religions, histories, and dozens of other factors. People's beliefs are deeply held – in many colonial countries I have seen a preference for lighter colour over darker, wealth over poverty, education over lack of literacy and numeracy, and so on. In fact such thinking gave rise to the caste system in eastern countries like India and the class system in western countries.

I have wondered if asking questions regarding where you came from are not just xenophobic but also spring from people's roots in working class life and values. In years gone by, when people in small villages met an 'outsider' they would ask the person where they were from and what they did for a living. As large sections of the population began to move to industrialised towns and people aspired to or joined the middle classes, they would ask questions such as where do you work, which school your children go to or which house of worship you attend. This was a way of categorising you – putting a label on your box or saying you are a specimen of a particular species.

We all know that humans fit into many categories and each category has different connotations or stereotypes associated with them. The stereotypes are not something each of us think up; they are derived from the thinking of our parents, communities and environments where we grow up or the media we are exposed to. Children absorb the way that people around them treat the stereotypes and then use those ways to handle stereotypes they come across as they grow up. It is unconscious. Perhaps it part of people's desire to establish a pecking order either to find their own place in relation to others or boost their egos and feel a sense of self-esteem, however fragile it be. And for many people, the problem may also lie in access to scarce resources. It may mean that being in a superior class, you may have first and unfettered access to resources such as jobs, homes, money, government positions.

But the theory about the scarcity of political resources driving racial and sexist resentment does not explain the whole phenomenon. Recent times have shown the rise of powerful white males to political life around the world. They are unwilling to share power and control with women. In these same countries, we see the rise of nationalism and extreme right-wing politics many of whom want to restore the primacy of the 'white' people. Analysts and expert opinion leaders say the reason is 'racial resentment', driven by a fear of losing status in a changing country, one in which the privilege of being a white man isn't what it used to be. It is a privilege under siege. An increasingly diverse society no longer accepts the God-given right of white males to run things. We now live in a society which has many empowered, educated women who are waking up and finally rejecting the privilege of *droit de seigneur* once granted to powerful men. An opinion leader believes it is about the rage of white men, upper class as well as working class, who perceive a threat to their privileged position.

Going back to the late nineteenth and early twentieth century history, some so-called scientists (more likely pseudo-scientists) believed that races existed as separate acts of creation. Some of these so called scientists invented theories to support their 'scientific racism', many of them publishing papers right up to the middle of the twentieth century that said some races were superior to others. Some were based on unscientific experiments which measured skull capacity or various parts of the body or applied skewed intelligence tests. Journal articles and photographic spreads in reputed magazines right up to the 1970's continued to portray black and brown people as exotics, natives and noble savages or domestic workers and labourers. Such portrayal reinforced the existing ideas of the time that the world was divided between the colonisers and the colonised and did little to shift existing stereotypes already ingrained in white Anglo-Celtic culture.

Racial distinctions continued to shape our politics, our neighbourhoods and our sense of self for many centuries. Later scientists have proved that most humans originated in North Africa and hence we all share the same genetic material. The mapping of the Human Genome over the past twenty or more years has also shown there is no genetic or scientific basis to the concept of race.

These so called scientific opinions regarding the intelligence and attributes of white and black people continues to surface into this century including words by prominent scientists who voice a personal and sometimes prejudiced opinion. One such prominent scientist is reported to have said that he found a difference between blacks and whites on average in IQ tests which he believed was genetic in nature! He also said that he disagreed with many social policies which he said were based on an assumption that the intelligence of black and white people were comparable. Such words have created a furore. Fortunately, many reputable scientists have come forward to castigate him for his unscientific and non-evidence based remarks.

Political and social reasons for racism and sexism: In Australia after the conclusion of World War II, a need for large-scale immigration was established which would include non-white people. Both conservative and more left-wing governments agreed on this and worked actively to dismantle such policies post-World War II to the nineteen-sixties. Technically, racism ended in the mid-1960's but people's attitudes often take much longer (years, if ever) to catch up with law. The Labor government elected in the early 1970's passed the Racial Discrimination Act 1975 to ensure that race would never be used as an excuse to exclude immigration from non-white countries. Government regulations to stop women from working in the Australian Public service were also revoked in the late 1960s, but sexism in corporate and public service departments existed for a long time. In 1984, Australia passed the Sex Discrimination Act and in the early 1990's, the Disability Discrimination Act, followed by the Age Discrimination Act in 2004. Laws do not change public attitudes and deeply held perceptions. All they can do is legislate certain behaviours, actions and words as illegal. In contrast, public attitudes can take a generation or more to catch up particularly if stereotypes remain embedded in society and people's own psyches are slow to change.

The concept of racism continues to be embedded in the structures, systems and institutions of our society's commercial, financial, political, media, educational and legal worlds. The top echelons in these spheres of public life are composed of white men such as CEOs to chairmen of commercial and financial corporations, politicians of all shades, and judges, lawyers and counsellors; owners and publishers of all kinds of print and electronic media as well as the movers and shakers of technology and communication. Such men (mostly men) issue statements and show preferences for articles, reporters, writers, theories which concur with their point of view. The systems of racism continue to be reinforced in books, speeches, advertising, movies, commonly used words and phrases. These are the frameworks we understand and use to interpret our social existence. The ideology and human figures at the top of all these 'food chains' subtly and overtly let us know how things stand. I do not imply that all people within large organisations and institutions are racist – but the power and control exerted by many of these systems and groups, often skewed and biased, makes them seem undeniably racist.

I recently read a statement in a book which said - we cannot have an honest reckoning about race until we start to recognise all the ways in which privilege and prejudice creep into our lives. When 'white' people give black or people of another colour 'backhanded compliments' such as 'you are so articulate' in a way that implies they are admiring you, it usually is a 'put-down', subtle as it may be. These are 'micro-aggressions and instances of casual racism that pepper our daily lives'. People like me have experienced this on an almost daily basis yet when we name it as racism, people become defensive. Racism may be easier to recognise and call out when people march around in white hoods or have swastikas on their arm-bands but not when they comprise every day casual put-downs and what I call patronising behaviour. It is our well-meaning friends, as I have discovered, who say 'but I am not racist – I have many black or brown or ethnic friends'. Just because you like 'black' or 'rap' music (or 'curry' dishes in my case), does not give you 'a free hall pass out of structural racism'. So many people I know do not know or accept the concept of 'white privilege'. They don't realise the privilege of being born white gives them a head-start from the starting line, something that is not available to people of colour or other ethnicities. Those who say they don't see race as an issue are saying 'there is nothing to fix'. Those who say they are 'colour-blind' or pretend blindness to racial issues perpetuate the system of oppression. Forced politeness or a fear of playing the 'race card' can stop progress or work towards an equitable and just future.

A recent documentary on Australian television showed a young Aboriginal girl being asked about her nationality. She told the audience that she was asked at a social function about her origins and when she told them she was Aboriginal, the questioner tried to reassure her by saying she was 'too pretty to be Aboriginal'! She said that people standing close by, who heard this put down, rolled their eyes and spoke condescendingly to her. She said she felt dirty and deeply shamed. I empathised with her in her feelings of shock when this young woman (like countless others of colour) receive back-handed compliments such as 'you are so articulate and exotic' or 'what percentage Aboriginal or Indian or Chinese are you?' We would not dream of saying to an Italian or German or Greek woman: 'you are too pretty to be Italian or German or Danish'. I am certain that women of colour and various ethnicities along with Aboriginal women, are measured against western beauty standards or racially exclusive ideals. We don't need to be interrogated about our identity because it is different to the prevailing norms of beauty or when juxtaposed against our place of origin. To say you are too pretty or too exotic or too smart to originate from whatever colour or tribe or ethnic origin you hail from is both racist and abusive and symptomatic of colonialism'. As a prominent activists in this field have remarked: ' I/We are not the problem!' Yes, the problem lies with the person making derogatory remarks based on personally-held stereotypical views of beauty, intelligence or whatever else is being demeaned.

Racism is more than prejudice and discrimination. Prejudice means judging someone because of their social or economic group or class origins and consists of feelings, thoughts, stereotypes and generalisations based on very little personal experience but projecting it on to a whole group. Prejudice is everywhere due to our acculturation and socialisation – absorbed from society at large. I have had people tell me that they were 'taught' not to be racist. I say that they were 'told' not to be racist because teaching would mean an inculcation of right standards at home and in society and all its structures. The socialisation that many of these people have received from their families, educational systems, government, political and economic systems and media, contain images and sub-texts - or prejudices and stereotypes - which they are unaware of until it is pointed out.

Racism is a combination of prejudice, discrimination and institutional power to perpetuate racial hierarchies. In my experience and observation, racism which includes racial hatred and tribalism is rising insidiously and obviously. Racism has never gone away but is morphing into new forms. Far right nationalist movements are to be seen in both western and eastern countries. Anti-immigrant and white supremacist groups are working openly in many countries and there seems to be a creeping acceptance of racism and bigotry in mainstream media and politics.

Then we have organisations and governments declaring that the people at the top have been put there because of 'merit'. I find the concept both egregious and laughable because merit has been decided by the people in power. A recent speech by a highly-regarded judge said that the idea of what constitutes "merit" is debatable and highly subjective. At its worst, it is the tendency to see **merit** "in those who exhibit the same qualities as the people on top or the ones in power, and can result in a perpetuation of homogeneity in hiring or appointments. Those of us who watch the people on top in parliament, the public service or the law see a preponderance of men over sixty, with grey hair and white skin – not truly representative of the society in which we live.

Other writers have said that talk of meritocracy is almost funny, a sort of roll-your-eyes type of in-joke. Some believe it is an undercurrent of political movement of males belonging to various in-clubs who perpetuate the image of people like themselves being at the helm of power at the expense of the general public. The irony lies in that the mythology of so-called merit which has been used to subdue and silence women in many political parties, medical and social clubs and in corporate life. When powerful political and corporate men invoke the holy grail of merit, it discourages women from acting collectively to advance their own interests. It says to women: form an orderly line, wait to be viewed or overlooked but don't complain afterwards, because no one likes a bitter, 'sour-grapes' woman. Many smart women have been taken in by such talk – they stay loyal to the prevailing corporate or political philosophy despite personal disappointments and experiences of being treated as outsiders. At the same time, the women who go along with the 'party-line' refuse to say they are feminists, even if they are so. They don't want to rock the boat or challenge the juggernaut-like machine, even as it rolls over and flattens them.

Ageism is also an insidious form of discrimination similar to sexism and racism. It involves prejudicial attitudes towards older people, old age, and the ageing process. Some say it is the next #MeToo. There has been a lot of recent media attention on older women in politics and power; however, in reality there is a vast number of older women in the workplace who are struggling to keep their jobs due to ageism and sexism. Many of these women suffer in silence when they are marginalized or subject to other ageist behavior, often passed over for leadership roles or pushed out. They are afraid to complain and draw attention to their age for fear they'll lose their jobs. The value and wisdom of older people is pushed aside and disparaged in our youth-oriented society; the emphasis is put on their 'senior moments', their inability to cope with changes to society including its new mores and technology. Attention is paid to the condition of their skin and health and their holding on to scarce economic resources. Stereotypes are used to describe older people – 'pruney', 'wrinkley',' oldie', 'old dear' or 'little man/woman'.

To return to the roots of racism and sexism. I say they lie at the heart of the ill treatment of women for centuries in every country of the world and doubly so for women of colour. Racism and sexism have also contributed to intergenerational trauma for women of all nationalities. Patriarchy has been embedded in just about every culture, way of life and almost all countries for many thousands of years. As a young woman studying English Literature, I was amazed to read a doggerel which dated to the times of Henry VIII (Tudor King of the mid-sixteenth century) which had words similar to this: a woman, a rug and a walnut tree, the more you beat them the better they be. Ownership of women, their bodies, any resources they may have owned or brought into a marriage/relationship was taken for granted and upheld by law - English, European, Indian, Middle Eastern, Asian. And women in some Eastern and Middle Eastern countries are still under male guardianship laws which prohibit them from following their own dreams and life goals. One writer described the domination and control of women as 'gender apartheid'. Additionally, domestic or family violence practiced to control and dominate women forms an egregious form of sexism. Countries and their rulers as well as religious men have been complicit in it.

THOUGHTS ON THE PSYCHOLOGY OF DISCRIMINATION

When we feel inadequate or insecure economically, physically, intellectually or emotionally we use the fight/flight mechanism, and often times discrimination or racist remarks become tools of attack. In those times of primal fear we revert to the unconscious mechanisms found or experienced in our childhood or socialisation. At such times, the very difference which could be celebrated and which is 'attractive' to a person who doesn't have that particular skin colour or gender, or intellectual skill becomes the weapon of hate and punishment.

When I see and hear ageism at work, I wonder if it has its roots in a fear of death and disability. Or do children and grandchildren perceive this as 'dependence' by their older relatives and resent it. Western society seems to adulate youth and beauty. When we avoid and reject older people and their value to society, we avoid thinking about or denying our own mortality.

Conscious or unconscious feelings of insecurity and fear – stemming from our feelings of inadequacy or believing we are less than others often start in childhood and in experiences growing up. It is the nature of Us and Them as seen in group dynamics. Insecurity often leads to the need to tear others down so as to raise ourselves up.

Those who have an 'inflated' **personal ego or a streak of narcissism** could think they have reason to look down on people different to them. This may include looking down on people with disabilities, or those who look (e.g. due to colour, gender, race) or behave differently (e.g. gay and intersex people) or those who are above or below us on the socio-economic ladder.

Being brought up in an insular family or community - Many of us were 'told' not to show prejudice or discriminate but we were not shown the benefits of valuing diversity or difference. All of us have heard the phrase – beauty is not skin deep! Most of us know that differences are natural and that none of us is better or worse than another based on superficial qualities such as skin colour or gender. However, if we have grown up hearing 'hate' or derogatory speech about people with different ethnicity, gender, sexuality or economic status or we have heard stereotypical descriptions applied to people different to us making them seem ridiculous and despicable then we become vulnerable when we find ourselves in situations which heightens our inadequacies and insecurities. This could happen if say we lost our job and discovered that a person of colour or another ethnicity was prospering.

Societal and peer pressure - We may have grown up in a community or society where discrimination and hatred of others was rampant. We are aware of wars in countries where ethnic cleansing may have taken place - people may have been killed or disappeared unless they subscribed to the ruling values. Such cleansing based on tribe, religion or skin colour allows the prevailing social order to stay intact because people see danger in diversity and difference. Hence, if our family, community, tribe held this particular sort of discrimination based on colour, place of birth, belonging to a social class as a matter of great esteem, even though we may have known or sensed that it was wrong, we feel the pressure to align with it. It is very powerful. But there are some people who would rather leave the planet than change. Change as a result of awareness we gain leads to authenticity and possibly reconciliation.

A large sporting organisation in this country recently apologised for racism shown to a recognised and accomplished Indigenous sportsman on the sporting field. This included booing and hissing and racist remarks about this great sportsman which sparked a vicious national debate about racism. It took years for the national sporting organisation to make an apology, perhaps prompted by the release of a documentary about this sportsman's life and achievements which included the overt racism he had experienced.

WHAT ABOUT UNCONSCIOUS BIAS?

Few of us are consciously sexist, racist or ageist. Many of us, modern, freedom-living, value-driven people have undertaken training programs, read a variety of articles, heard logical, fact-based arguments on radio and TV. As good human beings we have found ourselves getting sick of the same old argument. I have also watched the children of today who play and associate with kids of all races, religions, ethnicities that this would be an anathema to them.

So why so much talk about unconscious bias these days? Do all of us need more training as in the recent case of a large coffee chain and other organisations which are aiming to be good corporate citizens and create a culture which embraces differences? Yes, there I have said it – Diverse and inclusive!

Unconscious bias is part of this implicit thinking of which gender, race and ageist thoughts and stereotypes are sub-branches. Please remember it is not just sexist or racist people who have unconscious biases. In fact, most of us fair, human, equitable people have blind spots and some of these blind spots are about race, religion, age and gender. All of us have had different upbringings and lived in a disparate societies and communities and many of us still carry some form of gender, race and ageist norms, hang-ups and stereotypes.

Then there are experiences of unconscious bias which include being stereotyped as a 'little, native woman'. Let me explain. Recently, I was invited to address a seminar on women's rights and stood with a group of three women inside the door of the hall where the seminar would take place. Soon after a newcomer entered the group looking for more information but would not look at me, directing her enquiries to the white women standing on either side of me. I was puzzled initially; I was sure I had spoken knowledgeably on the subject but felt my dark skin may have sent out a message saying I am ignorant, uneducated and could not possibly feel and speak passionately on such as subject.

I have heard similar accounts from women of colour, one of whom is a professor of mathematics at a renowned university and hails from a south Asian country. She told her audience wearily that most times she is taken to be a cleaner/janitor or one of the catering staff at various events she is invited to attend. Such assumptions included a time when she walked up the red carpet at a large event to collect a rare international prize in mathematics; she was asked by the security guard to go around to the serving staff entrance. Another woman, who is married to a corporate executive of south-Asian origin and speaks excellent English, told me similar accounts of being at restaurants where she is asked by the wait-staff for her choice of meals and wines while her husband is ignored, attracting bland, slippery gazes. I call this particular gaze, which seems to slither over me or other people of colour, the 'gaze of grease'! People who do this seem to hold a deep belief or stereotypical view that all people of colour are either illiterate or semi-literate and need to be treated with the kid gloves of patronage. These people forget that their micro-expressions and lack of engagement with people of colour betray their inner thoughts and feelings.

Asking people where they are from may not seem discrimination to you – but it is intrusive when you stare at their brown, black, polka-dotted skin and think it is different and ask your curiosity-laden question! Perhaps it is your way of trying to reach out to them but to the person at the receiving end of the question, it feels insensitive, unsophisticated, and 'excludes' the person facing you. It achieves the opposite of 'inclusiveness' and 'diversity' which corporate, community people and politicians want. Most of us would not direct such questions to a person with an obvious disability or someone with paralysis across half their face or a huge birthmark because our compassion tells us that it is both intrusive and unkind. So please spare a thought for people who face this question almost daily, who believe they are now part of the larger community but discover their comfortable citizenship is questioned to satisfy your curiosity.

My personal awareness has grown as I have matured and developed first-hand knowledge of communities and their customs and traditions. But I have also known too many 'white' people to: firstly, not appreciate the origins of this (Australia's) land or its peoples and secondly, to remain unaware of the long cultural heritage that comes with it. There are some who don't understand the term 'Acknowledgement of Country' (when given by a non-Indigenous person or a person not from the local clan) or 'Welcome to Country' (normally a greeting given by an Aboriginal elder on the land/place where the meeting takes place). Many Anglo-Celtic citizens of this land seem to come unstuck when they realise that the Aboriginal or Indigenous people of this country are the true owners of this land not the white people who have usurped the ownership and heritage of dark-skinned people. Now I say to those who ask "where are you from": "I am an immigrant just like you." This is part of the bridge to equity and understanding that I believe we need to build as we work and live in this land.

We often hear the truism: We are a multi-cultural nation and we love the diversity and richness that people of all colours, ethnicities, sexual preferences, and cultures this brings! I believe we are not a truly multi-cultural society but on the way to becoming one sometime in the future. In the meantime, we are a collection of microcosms of multiculturalism and ethnic groups, not living in ghettos but afraid to venturing out too freely. Please remember - multiculturalism, ethnic diversity and gender preferences are more than 'buzz' words. People of colour or various ethnic groups or those who prefer to be identified by another gender are not exotic animals to be collected for some superficial idea of valuing multiculturalism and diversity. As people we are more than the sum of people with certain ethnic foods or appearing in 'national' costumes and dancing for Harmony day (when countries celebrate the ethnic and racial diversity of people) or appearing in a Mardi Gras parade. Nor are people of colour - black, brown, brindle or Indigenous or people who have chosen another gender identity - personal mascots that can be worn on your cap or sleeve to tell others how gracious and equity-minded you are. Please don't let social insensitivity in digging out people's ethnic origins or changes in sexual identity get the better of you. Instead, think of ways that will allow you to bring them into your inner circle as friends and equal human beings. I invite you to reach out and build a bridge so that we can all come to a place of mutual respect and inclusiveness.

I heard a Slam poet recently whose poem spoke to my heart. We only open up to our friends – not people who accost us on the street or the train or we meet at a party. We reveal our innermost selves, our thoughts and experiences in all their fullness and the painful details of our lives when we know people are not prying to satisfy their curiosity but because they really care for us as friends and want to see us as whole human beings.

My **purpose in writing** this book, one that has nagged me for years, has been to give voice to the subjects that are avoided and often tucked away - racism, sexism, ageism, misogyny and patriarchal control in marriage and religion. I wanted to bring these topics to our awareness and consciousness. I did not want the subjects to become the proverbial elephant in the room that we tiptoe around hoping others will understand. What I have found that though the currents of racism, sexism and violence towards women were deep subjects I was told to avoid, ultimately they were shallow in the face of a real, authentic humanity.

However, change is only possible when we recognise the hurt and harm our behaviour or thinking has caused. We cannot solve problems unless we are conscious of how they arose, the events that led up to it, what happened along the way and the harm they have caused. It is only when we recognise the roots of the problem and how it arose, and resolve to find a way forward that change begins to happen a little at a time.

I want us to be friends wherever we are – globally or locally - who make an effort to understand and respect each other. I want us to build bridges of deep knowledge, understanding and support with those we meet or already know before we begin to pick on scabs or open new wounds. There is so much that connects us as human beings – far more than the things that divide us – whether this is skin colour, race or gender identity amongst a host of so called differences.

The issues and beliefs that divide us threaten our existence. As humans we are more connected than we realise both today and in our ancient genetic past. Our survival as a species and a universal tribe of humanity means finding common solutions and bases of understanding than weapons and schisms that would divide us.

THE PEOPLE WHO INFLUENCED ME

Lessons from my father and grandfather

I need to acknowledge the debt to my parents and grandparents (whose life stories are contained towards the end of this book) for an upbringing that was founded on ethical and social values, many derived from Christianity though most from an ordinary respectful humanity. I also laud my father's values which came from a pan-Indian Hindu philosophy of tolerance. They took the moral and social education of a child seriously – not by way of lectures – but mostly through stories and experiences from their own lives and sharing the wisdom they had obtained from these.

I learnt valuable lessons regarding leadership. Modest, compassionate leadership – sometimes from the front and often from behind like a form of stewardship. Their roles/jobs were vastly different – my grandfather was a leader in community service, people and social welfare; my father was a high-ranking army leader. Both strategised and evaluated the results of their strategy even if it was months and years later. Their strategy was always marked with ways to operate fluidly and to learn from their mistakes. They laughed at their own stumbles and their wins. Many times I heard their humility, self-deprecation, kindness, yet a valiant sticking to their ethics and high moral standards. I think the latter is what stands out in my mind as the basis for all they did.

Another point: they never called attention to their achievements or successes and that remains a big factor in my life – never to blow my own trumpet even if people choose to pull you down or ridicule you and your achievements. I am told by people who watch me in leadership roles that I act 'too humble'. I am bewildered. What other way is there? I believe in stewardship and leading gently and cooperatively. I think the so-called charismatic leadership of politicians today is based on grandiosity and narcissism.

Like my father and maternal grandfather, I think of myself as someone who seeks to employ any power I possess or privilege I have for a common good. I wish I had the power to change the world But I seek to change, at ground or community level, the fate of women and the helpless and homeless, the power to soothe and give sustenance to those who do not have as much as I have. I believe this is part of my self-actualisation and my belief in our common universality. It is the inheritance I want to leave behind for those I know or have been privileged to come into contact with - women, people with disability, people of colour and various ethnicities, down-trodden men and women whom we see in the homeless, the powerless, and the new migrants and refugees - to achieve their heart's desire

Lessons from my mother and grandmother

The values of giving and helping and various forms of social justice that I saw in my grandmother's and mother's lives have served me well. I learnt many good principles and concepts from the Christianity that they practiced which had humanity at its core. My early upbringing and the values instilled by these women helped me to keep compassion very much top of mind and heart. It helped me to care for people without being judgemental of their situation or their particular beliefs. I also discovered the value of empathy.

Their examples have helped to keep speaking my truth with courage even when people around me seem to be saying or going down opposite paths. Fearlessness is not easy but it gets easier as you practice it. Courage along with having a compassionate heart. I remember my grandmother's words: 'Never tamp down the compassion welling up in your heart'.

During my upbringing, I heard the words of Jesus, Aristotle and Socrates were as meaningful as the lives of Jewish prophets and kings and the words of the Christian apostles. I also heard concepts of Hindu philosophy from the *Bhagvad Gita*, *Ramayana* and the *Upanishads* along with the writings of Muslim sages such as Kabir, Rumi, Hafiz and Khayyam. Additionally, I was brought up on a diet of stories and examples from English, Hindu and Muslim literature that were available at that time. We were exhorted to grow up as fine, upright and compassionate human beings to whom others would look up to as community luminaries.

The Christian upbringing received from my mother and grandmother has led me to admire the character and values of Jesus Christ. The Sermon on the Mount (Matthew Chapters 5 to 7, KJV) remains as a monument to loving, just and humane principles. The golden rule of behaving towards others as we expect them to behave towards us (Matthew 7:12 KJV) and also found in most of the world's religions remains one of my basic ways to live my life. I also found that Christ not only cared for the poor and down-trodden but also honoured women even though he lived in and was brought up in a patriarchal culture and society. I also admire his distaste for hypocritical and prejudiced people; I love his plain-speaking ways and refusal to disavow his core beliefs.

I remember and have reacquainted myself with some of Aristotle's philosophy – that ethical virtues such as justice, courage, compassion and kindness are central to a well-lived life. He believed that complex rational, emotional and social skills cannot be acquired through training in the sciences, mathematics and philosophy or a discursive understanding of goodness. You can only get them through proper upbringing and habits and the ability to see the course of action that is best supported by reason. Practical wisdom does not come by learning general rules. We actually need to acquire these through practice, through continuous use of emotional and social skills.

My parents and grandparents laid the foundation stones of justice, equality, leadership leavened with kindness and compassion in me. They led me on my journey of struggle to find equity and justice in a global modern society. It led me to climbing the ladder in the corporate world over forty years ago. They inspired me to educate myself further and learn to speak with courage and confidence. The journey led me to the C-Suite despite the intransigence and discrimination of people who thought I would not be able to do the job but I produced huge outcomes

Being down and out when I arrived in Australia was a blessing in disguise. Pushing through obstacles formed my character and left an indelible mark on my psyche. I have grown stronger and 'richer' in every way.

WHAT I HAVE LEARNT FROM MY DAUGHTER AND A NEW GENERATION

Teaching and working with younger people – at least a generation or two after me - has opened my eyes to the value of being connected and building bridges of understanding and transparency so as to give them a sense of the past but also open their hearts and minds to the daily learning they are exposed to. Technology and widespread social media communication have made us a smaller world not a bigger one.

I have learnt that it is important that education not only include the three Rs – reading, writing and arithmetic - but also the three Cs of creativity, communication and collaboration. To this let us add a huge dose of understanding and a desire for change. The younger generation demonstrate to us daily that they take social and civic responsibility seriously and they will use all the tools of digital literacy and their access and usage of a huge range of social networks to liven our consciences. Young children in primary school access knowledge and act with decency and respect to people outside their immediate network in causes such as Indigenous traditional ownership, climate change, respect for LGBTIQ people or the women's movement.

I have learnt so much from people younger than myself - children, teenagers, young adults – new ways of looking at all manner of cultural, social and political issues e.g. taking care of the environment, respecting people from all ethnicities and personal persuasions, the rights and need for support by LGBTIQ, homeless and refugee people.

These and other topics of conversation with my daughter over a number of years have created an impetus in me to keep learning and growing on a range of subjects from the rights of traditional Indigenous owners of Australia, to those of people with a disability, to housing and care for the homeless and the aged, and the rights and needs of refugees and asylum -seekers. Dialogues about Indigenous people and migrant and refugee women's rights have become springboards to gather further knowledge and engage in action. These areas fire my own vitality and passion for justice and action.

MY FATHER - AN 'OFFICER AND A GENTLEMAN'

I thought I had an ordinary life till I grew up and discovered that we were either unique or perhaps an odd and eccentric family. Socially, culturally, my parents were miles apart in their outlook and beliefs. India is a large and diverse sub-continent and my parents came from opposite parts of the country – a thousand to fifteen hundred miles apart . That my parents both lived in one continent - or different parts of India –did not make them typically Indian. You may as well say that a Swedish man and a Greek woman are European because they live on the same continent though a thousand miles apart. My parents did not speak the same language, did not have the same religion and their societal culture was very different. My father was a Hindu man, born into a very high caste Brahmin family in southern India. His father had been a devout Hindu and spent his life as a High School Maths teacher, like his own father who had also been a Maths teacher. Dad was a very intelligent man which included being excellent at mathematics but he did not want to be a teacher like his father's and grandfather's footsteps or a priest like the rest of their clan. Nor did he want to be a gold merchant like some of his forebears. He loved adventure and excitement, so shortly after leaving High School and attending a year at college (university), he quit academic study despite his father's pleas and threats. He went off to try his fortune as wars raged (World War II) and India reached the zenith of its struggle for independence. The world wars and people's struggle to be independent of colonialism brought promises of equality and liberty to the forefront of many people's minds.

Dad was born in 1919 shortly after World War I ended. He was named after a Hindu god who had a temple dedicated to his name in his native town. This was a long and arcane name so I have called him Raj. As tradition required, he incorporated his father's name and the name of their family's ancestral village into his name. It was a long, multi-syllabic name which he would later shorten for ease of use by his military and civilian colleagues as well as my mother. He was born in small town India but his emotional, mental and philosophical base was anything but small town Indian. As he grew and learnt and absorbed the *zeitgeist* of his times, his education and beliefs and way of life became very cosmopolitan.

Raj was the oldest of five brothers and one sister and was brought up by a father who felt it was his duty and responsibility as well as the mores of their caste and community to set a good example. The five boys toed the line as dictated by their father but the experience of growing up under his father's rigid ways was very hard and even traumatic for him. The world was changing around him post World War I and the small town in southern India where he had grown up also felt the effects of the winds of change that were beginning to affect all parts of the globe. As a teenager and young man, he loved and wanted to experience everything new and was a daredevil in more ways than one. He loved the movies (Hindi, Tamil and English) and the world to which this exposed him. He told me that one of his favourite movies was called 'Anarkali' with a dialogue in Hindi (a language he barely understood) but he fell in love with the female actor and saw it nineteen times.

He was not content to stay within the boundaries and rules of his community or those imposed by his rigid and domineering father. At school and at home, he rebelled against the rules and regulations imposed on him – from eating the vegetarian food given him by his parents to his Brahmin-imposed tonsure. He also found a group of friends which included Christian and Muslim boys because they seemed different or 'exotic'. The group became best mates much to the chagrin and anger of his father who thought he would literally beat the disobedience and stigma of associating with non-Brahmins and non-Hindus out of him. I am told, my grandfather would tie him to a pillar in their home and 'beat' him with iron chains when he found out about his 'transgressions' such as his friendships with non-Hindu boys or shaving his head to change his distinctive Brahmin tonsure. But nothing stopped my father from doing as he chose though it must have traumatised him. Perhaps it made him more determined to 'slip the chains' of cruelty and follow his own heart and path.

My paternal grandfather's rage, which drove him to whip Dad with chains to keep him away from Muslim and Christian boys at school was derived from his need to protect and keep his elite Brahmin name and caste pure. This seems to be in stark contrast to my grandfather's philosophical ideals; he belonged to the 'Quit India' movement started by Gandhi, which was against British rule and wanted Indians of every denomination to be free and equal. The winds of change were blowing gustily in the first half of the twentieth century with world wars and the rise of various 'isms' like communism, democracy and the need for equality and would continued to change for the entire century and into the next one.

Dad's mother was a beautiful and placid woman who felt her main role in life was to cook, clean and mother the children but she gave her tough and inflexible husband full latitude to lay down the law with his family. I was never able to speak to her when I got to meet her in my late teens except through smiles and loving looks because she could not speak the languages I could – English, Hindi, Urdu – and I could not speak her only language – Tamil.

Dad's favourite brother was the middle one who was ten years younger. Their bond was strong. This brother was 'adopted' (at age five) by a cousin of my grandfather, who had no children of his own, and went to live in their village forty miles away. Dad missed him and would make the journey every couple of weeks to this village by thumbing lifts from passing trucks. This bond would stay strong throughout their lives. His other brothers adored their older brother who went on to make good and have a great and glorious life. Even in their forties and fifties, they remained in awe of him and his exploits.

Dad's uncle (his father's brother) was very fond of him though he had children of his own. I think it was the adventurous, free spirit that drew them to each other. This uncle was a trader and jeweller and worked alongside his brother (my grandfather, the Maths teacher) in their family home and business. The family normally entered careers in education, in line with their priestly/academic heritage, and other members of the family worked in their small jewellery business. (I have often wondered if the love of education and jewellery has been baked into my genes.) Dad's uncle taught him to swim and drive via the 'throw him in and let him survive' method. Dad was thrown into a big well so as to learn how to swim, then into a huge pond, called a tank, attached to a temple. Dad's introduction to cars was similar – he found himself behind a car belonging to his uncle's friend. He watched the friend drive this manual machine and then, when no one was watching, took off with a friend sitting beside him with much grinding of gears, kangaroo jumps and honking of horns. He did learn quickly and soon became an accomplished but fast driver. It was to be among the skills he owned up to when he joined the Royal Indian Air Force.

He left home shortly after finishing a year at College when he was nineteen, moving to a big city close by and spending time doing odd jobs from being a petrol station attendant to driving cars for whoever asked him to. Shortly after, World War II began and India, as a British 'colony', was swept into the War. Indian troops lined up to enlist and went to fight in exotic places far away from their native India.

Most Indians wanted a job earning money for their families and their motivation was not to serve their British King and the empire. Indians had supported the movement of civil disobedience and wanting self-governing status started by one of the founding fathers of Indian patriotism after World War I when Britain refused to honour its promise given during the first War about India having 'dominion' and limited self-rule status. The winds of change and independence were sweeping the country as people like Gandhi took long journeys on foot trying to bind Hindus, Muslims and other faiths together in a movement to claim India for Indians. The British masters responded slowly though a few saw the writing on the wall. Some of their actions included a limited form of 'self-rule' in certain areas of the country. They also came up with a form of 'Affirmative Action' when they discovered the need to arm a large army against the Axis powers as they engaged in World War II.

With his quick-wits and having a risk-loving nature, he joined the Royal Indian Air Force in the middle of World War II as a non-commissioned officer. He took to his role and duties quickly and decided the military would be his life and career. Two years later, he was selected to go before the Officers Selection Board, which I understand the panel was made up of a lot of loyalist, patriotic and stiff-upper-lip British officers. When asked why he wanted to be part of the military and the officer cadre, he replied 'To make a career for myself and my family'. His truthful remarks impressed the Board as did his education, his intelligence, his mechanical and mathematical skills, his command of the English language and (most of all, I think) his love of all things English. Yes, he was an Anglophile to his very bone marrow. So he became an officer in the Air Force and learnt to fly planes and do many wild and rakish things such as cutting corn with the wing tips of the planes he flew. He was given all the accoutrements of a British officer including his own personal batman and access to the Officers Mess. In turn he learnt all the finer points of alcohol, European food, and the traditions, rituals, etiquette and manners befitting an English officer along with the necessary training to be an officer commanding 'native' troops.

He quickly moved around the Indian sub-continent - wherever there was an expectation of Japanese invasion or action. He became the quintessential Englishman- an officer and a gentleman – mostly by osmosis. He was one of a small cadre of Indian men who were being trained by the British government and army to take over the military when they left India, men who would keep the received British traditions and behave with dignity. Apparently, the British had adopted this philosophy ever since the late 1930's when they came to realise that India would become independent of British rule sooner or later. I think they wanted a loyal group of men who loved all things British and would behave in a similar manner. I feel sad to say that the efforts of these loyal Indian men and women have been largely forgotten by white men and women (in Britain, Europe and Australia). The natives supported their British and European masters to win World Wars. They were quickly co-opted into the war and just as quickly forgotten afterwards.

As World War II was ending, Raj was sent to a town in northern India where he met my mother, Kusum – a young woman of 20, a Christian woman who was subtly being taught to be free and independent thinking by her parents.

What was unique or odd about Dad? Born in a traditional Hindu upper caste family, he managed to escape the excruciating bonds of his caste and religion. Like him, I believe the caste system is synonymous with inequality and is a form of exploitation. It needs to be dismantled from the top down and bottom up as many Indians have done over the past seventy-odd years. His brothers did not have the same fierce will to 'individuate' and live their truth – much as they hero-worshipped him and secretly admired his independence and free-thinking mind. His open-mindedness led him to marry a woman he loved though she belonged to another religion and was not from his high caste. It also led him to bring up his children to believe in the values of equality and fairness.

I believe he must have wanted some amount of regulation and boundaries in his life, in line with the strict but hateful upbringing by his autocratic father, so he chose the military life. That gave him structure but it also allowed him to find his place and meaning in life. He loved the military life and the British upper-class style of living because it allowed him to mix with intelligent, educated and forward-thinking men and women. Thus he could really, truly find himself or to the extent that the free world of the time permitted him. He soon learned and acquired the tastes that appealed to him. He loved the parades, the medals, pips and signs of his rank on his epaulettes, the regimen and the regiment and so on. To this day, I find myself getting teary-eyed when I see military bands marching to martial music as I often do on Australia Day or Anzac Day or when I watch the Changing of the Guard. The moment the music starts, particularly bagpipe music, I am transported back to age seven or eight, sitting or standing along with other army children or families in a marquee watching troops march past in uniform with accompanying bands. My experiences date to a time which was immediately after the British left India but the military traditions they had inculcated in the rank and file of the army stayed on. He loved the army life and I know he would have loved to have died as a soldier in a high position, died with his boots on.

In stark contrast, my mother who had been brought up also by a father, who loved all things British and European, and enjoyed much of the life-style, manners, education and upbringing suitable for an upper-middle-class Englishwoman actually hated the military life because it came to represent a gypsy existence – from town to town and cantonment to cantonment. In line with his lively, risk-loving nature Dad always opted for assignments and positions which took him to active fighting fronts where families were neither allowed nor could live safely or with the conveniences provided by larger cities. I think she was more free-thinking philosophically but her heart and mindset was not attuned to the way that Dad enjoyed in life. She was also shy to a large extent whereas Dad was an extrovert and a man full of dash and bravado. All life was a 'dare' – dare to jump in and swim an icy cold river, cut wheat or corn with his plane's wingtips, join a parachute troop regiment and jump as often as he could. He did the latter with panache and style till he broke his leg in a particular jump in thirteen places and was 'grounded' for six months, causing him to transfer to the Artillery Corps -another action-packed division of the army .

He was a quick-thinking, chameleon of a man able to find a way to explain situations to his advantage. During his army career, he always had a batman (called an orderly in the Indian army) to keep his uniform and personal belongings in order. One of them was a soldier who followed him (or Dad got him transferred) when he changed units or regiments. He was faithful to Dad and devoted to us children. His fellow soldiers would often say that he was like a second mother to us – perhaps because he had none of his own on whom he could lavish affection and care. This batman was to develop mental health issues later in life over his inability to have children. When he went back on a month's furlough he saw another man's shoes outside his own little home, guessed that according to the tradition of his particular clan that some fertile young man was being brought in to make his wife pregnant. He turned around, went back to the railway station and came back to be at Dad's side but his mind had been bruised and he would spend many years in a military psychiatric hospital.

The next orderly was neither as loyal or dedicated to his duties as the former one. Shoes were left half-polished, uniforms not hung properly, brass pips on epaulettes stayed half-tarnished and so on. But his major downfall was yet to come. On one occasion, he packed Dad's uniform and accoutrements for a tour of army units in distant parts of the state but forgot to put his belt in. When Dad woke in the morning in this distant town and started to dress in order to take a parade, he realised that there was no belt for his uniform. Not wearing a belt is equivalent to saying that the person is under arrest. He opted to wear his civilian clothes to attend his military duties. He did this with panache making up an excuse of needing to go and see some government staff. He rang my mother and complained about this and asked that I should be put in charge of packing his clothes and ensuring that all the requisites were present. I was then the sharp-witted, clever, all-knowing child of the older three siblings. At fifteen years of age, I became Dad's part-time orderly or batman or the batman's supervisor. His batman continued in his job for a few more months until he made another mistake – he put one of Dad's shoulder pips upside down. This was noticed by a fellow officer when Dad went to the Officer's Mess in the afternoon for a beer and the resulting traditional 'punishment' was called on – standing a round of drinks for everyone in the mess (a financial punishment). This was the second and last chance for this man and he was replaced by someone else though I remained the supervisor of batmen and Dad's wardrobe.

Dad had at least twelve pairs of shoes or more including boots, wellingtons, dress shoes etc. and a fair amount of clothes including uniforms and suits for a man of that time and era. Very likely this was due to his rank and military career. I wonder if this put the thought in my head that I needed a multitude of clothes and shoes suited for every occasion and need like he did. I became a clothes horse and shoe-addict like a famous Filipina first lady. I know I did not get that love or fixation on clothes from my mother or my grandparents on either side. I have also wondered if my love of clothes could be linked to my creativity as a child and teenager when I designed and made my own and my sister's clothes. Or was it due to my 'want' during the years of being economically controlled by my first husband?

I also inherited or perhaps absorbed his style of interior decor – things rich and beautiful-looking - yet with an overall theme of magnificence without fuss and frills. Where did that come from? Very likely his tastes were moulded along the lines of the India that the British had loved – opulent, magnificent, full of colour, unique and sometimes eccentric. However, the British who had lived in India had gotten the taste from the Rajahs and Maharajahs. The latter had lived in that style with gorgeous fabrics, bright colours, splendid furniture and unusual household things. Dad did not care for pale and neutral looks – they were too insipid for him. I feel the same way as he did and love gorgeous colours, unconventional but Eastern-looking decor and art in all forms that suits my taste and decorating style. When I see movies and books highlighting the days of the British Raj and showing gorgeous, colourful homes and gardens, I find tears of nostalgia welling up and a lump inmy throat. I think the richness and glory of British clubs and officers' messes always reminded him of the life of a Rajah or a high-ranking British aristocrat. He carried forward his initiation and immersion in that glorious life, remaking new homes in army cantonments that we moved to. Any Officers' messes or Clubs over which he may have had influence were decorated and run in the same magnificent vein.

What I remember most is his leadership style. Gracious, quick-witted, leading from the front without being proud or arrogant. In a country, where people from different states and language groups stuck together, he was feted and admired by north Indian men in his military career. Despite his south Indian birth with a very different native language, he learnt to speak Hindi and Punjabi well and made his life in the northern India, speaking and mixing with troops and officers and conversing with them in English and north Indian languages.

One of his stand-out features was his honesty and incorruptibility. At a time, when one of the recruiting arms was being beset by tales of corruption, he was sent by one of the senior generals to 'sort it out'. He brought order and high standards to an arm of the military which was sliding backwards. Once this clean-up or cleanout was over, he returned to active service with the regiment of artillery, which had been his passion for most of his army career.

After three years of restoring order in a non-frontline role, he learnt that he was to be promoted to the rank of Brigadier. His greatest accomplishment was yet to come. He took over command of an Artillery brigade in a far northern town not far from the western border. Just a year later, war broke out and Dad was soon in his element as he prepared for battle though my mother, two sisters and younger brother were not. In fact, they were traumatised. They continued to live in this town very close to the border because Dad had promised my mother that he would not let any harm come to them.

They continued to live there while tracer rockets flew overhead, guns boomed day and night, reconnaissance planes flew low and the backyard had trenches for them to hide in. The younger two siblings had issues with planes for many years – my sister opting to have the shortest showers in history because whenever she went into the shower, an air-raid alarm sounded. My younger brother took to hiding under beds when this happened. The trauma was to affect both of them; my sister to be hyper-vigilant with some elements of PTSD which she manages to control well. It is our youngest sibling who has developed symptoms of various sorts as he has grown older- PTSD, bi-polar behaviour, with some autism and aggression. I think there is a combination of and overlapping layers of all those conditions.

Dad got a war time promotion to the rank of Major General which he cherished. But his military career was not to last forever; my mother had finally lost her nerve and wanted to get out of army life and Dad finally succumbed to her pressure. He decided to quit the army just when he had got to the level and position of where he wanted to be.

If someone were to ask me which parent I am like and whose tastes I share, I would say Dad. We had much in common though as a young child or teenager I was not his favourite. He doted on my older sister, which would annoy me intensely. (Such is the intensity of sibling rivalry and hurt.) However, for a man brought up in a traditional Indian family, he loved his daughters – my older sister first, then my younger sister, who was the apple of his eye. Only after I left home at age eighteen, did we begin to get on as friends. It was only in my middle-age that he began to see me for the person I was. And I began to appreciate the man and father that he had been. I feel sad that we have to go through our own maturation process and stumble in our own efforts at parenting to appreciate the love and difficulty experienced by our parents.

I had a quick mind and way with words like him. We would argue over the dinner table on various subjects such as Sino-Soviet foreign policy or the value of a generic brand versus a specific product. He also had a great eye for beautiful things and taught himself interior decoration following the magnificent Maharajah style. Somehow I imbibed this from him and we discovered that our decorating styles were so similar as to be identical at times. Where should we place the furniture and hang the artwork that we carried around from place to place? What colour and sort of fabric should be used for the drapes? What should the colour of paintwork on the walls and architraves? And how should we landscape the garden – a fountain here and flower-beds there? No one taught him what to do but he had some inner sense of what looked good and stylish (a combination of grand-maharaja-British-colonial) There were times when my mother would argue with him about colour and furniture placement but he had discovered that we had similar tastes. He would call me over and say he wanted to consult with me, his Artistic Director, then proceed to ask: 'So where would you put these pieces of furniture or how should we hang these paintings?' And without fail, I would give views identical to his. My mother insisted he had coached me but it was not true. Just strange and coincidental.

Despite his rise to high rank in the army (Brigadier-General) he was a modest man and never trumpeted his achievements or heroics. He did not use his rise to high office in the army to lord it over others or expect people to be subservient to him. At the peak of his career, he met one of his school friends who was also in the army and was delighted to see him after many years. Dad was in civilian clothes that day at a gymkhana and his friend boasted that he had now made Major and went on to tell about his exploits and achievements. He gave him many a good-natured jab and threw his arm around Dad's shoulders as he chattered on. After a while, he asked, 'And what do you do now?' And Dad answered, 'I look after a brigade in my spare time!' The arm around his shoulder was jerked off hastily as his friend began to apologise for taking liberties. But such was his charm and modesty that he continued talking to him and invited him over for lunch to our place.

My father stayed a Hindu for over thirty years after meeting my mother albeit an agnostic one. Apparently, he had promised my mother when they married that he would not force her to change her religion though I think she had not promised the same in return. She always tried to get him to 'convert' but he was devoted to his military career, his agnosticism and not interested in conversion.

He left the army and took up civilian life in his late forties but not with the same gusto. I think he felt the need to support and please my mother, who had followed him around the country-side for the first twenty-five or thirty years of their married life. He worked as a general manager for an engineering firm, then as regional manager for the south-Asian branch of a European manufacturing and marketing company. The civilian life in India lasted for close to ten years by which time, my mother and older sister convinced him to go and live in USA so that they could all live close to each other. He gave in but I think he always looked back with fondness to his military career where he had climbed the heady peaks of success, in a way he had never imagined.

Arriving in USA, my father who had never depended on anyone for help decided to take up a minor administrative role in a bank so as to support his own pared-down family. He continued working in the role for ten years right up to age seventy-five never being a burden to any one or asking anyone for a handout. Dad had to learn to take 'orders' from low level bureaucrats when he had commanded brigades of fifteen to twenty thousand men in India and later overseen a regional business. I believe he wanted to feel independent and make a niche of friends for himself and my mother. He never lost his intelligence, sharpness or wit till the day he died at age 88.

I think I got most of my ambition and fearlessness from Dad as well as his intelligence and ability to interact with wit and perspicacity at all levels of society. He was committed to equity as seen by his refusal to ditch his Christian and Muslim friends whom he met at High school and whom his father had forbidden him to mix with. I think this is partly what drew him to my mother – a beautiful Christian woman. The strange and exotic was powerful to him... also the forbidden fruit. He was the son of a Brahmin man with a long line of academic and priestly ancestors but he refused to be bound by religion or caste or people's station in society. His chosen career allowed him to love British military traditions such as he found in the Air Force originally and then in the Indian army. Like his father-in-law, he became a firm believer in women's emancipation and education and supported them in following a career and an independent life. In that sense, he was a 'feminist' because he did not treat his daughters any differently to his sons and supported them in their education, careers and life decisions to fulfil their dreams.

MY MOTHER - THE GOLDEN TIGRESS

'A person of excellent qualities is like a flower, which whether found amongst weeds or worn on the head still preserves its fragrance' says an old Indian proverb

My mother, whom I shall call Kusum, was born in 1924, the second daughter in the family, and it was generally believed that she would lead a charmed life. She was named after a wonderful sweet-smelling tropical flower, which grew in the family garden. Indian poets have written of the beauty and fragrance of this magical flower and its use in worshipping the gods.

The images of fragrant flowers dancing upon newly budded leaves have been described by poets bring back many fond memories. My sister and I included lines from the poets about this flower in my mother's memorial eulogy document to give to mourners at her funeral service; we also lightly sprayed the document and the mourners, as they wished, with a wonderful and expensive perfume, where the base note contains the essence of Indian magnolia flowers.

My mother and her older sister, named after a revered Hindu demi-goddess, were loved and wanted by their parents who had determined that they would be brought up with a good education, excellent social manners and be inculcated in all things Christian. This was most unusual for their time and the society they lived in. Women were not educated to any level – the majority of women in that day and age probably did not even have a primary school education; they were not allowed independent thinking and speech and their lives, marriages and social interactions were strictly dictated. Their upbringing was very different to the India they lived in – with its gods and goddesses and beliefs in mystery, *maya* and mythology. Years later when I was born, Dad named me after a goddess, who danced at the court of the gods and brought wealth and wisdom to her devotees. Names of gods, goddesses and ancient Hindu kings would reverberate in our family for years to come.

My mother and her siblings were part of a family which could be described as more English than Indian. India was under British rule but my grandfather was enamoured of all things British and German. The cleanliness, organisation, so-called humanity and compassion of the rulers, educational and social values and mores spread by the British rulers were heaven-sent to him. He inhaled these values and manners and made them his own and soon the family was also living as an upper-class Indian family or an upper-middle-class British family. They had household attendants for everything – maids to clean and a nanny to look after children, a male steward/cook, a butler, a gardener and his assistant, a chauffeur and before that a coach-driver for their horse and carriage. Their home, which consisted of many bedrooms and living areas was cleaned twice daily; food was served in their dining room by a butler and/ or a maid; their clothes were washed and cleaned daily; their bed linen washed and delivered to their home by a *dhobi* (washerman) twice a week. The gardener and his assistant looked after the vast gardens, planting annuals and perennials, cutting lawns and tending a vegetable garden; coachman with a horse-driven carriage took them to school and picked them up later, often driving their mother and the children to shop or visit friends. Their world was a garden of privilege and of flowers. The family colloquially referred to its first home as 'Heart's Delight' and when they moved to another huge home, my grandfather began to refer to it as the Nightingale's Nest (verbalising his wish for generations of children to sing and play in its gardens).

For a woman who had been born in the first quarter of the twentieth century in a land which was just beginning to come out of a lack of education, freedom and access to human rights particularly female rights, my mother had an unusual and liberal upbringing. Her parents were inspired by the new social and moral values including a belief in women's education and the right of women to speak openly and without asking for permission. Like her own mother, Kusum was sent to English speaking private schools along with her older sister and she excelled at all subjects including English, History, and Mathematics. She finished High School, matriculation as it was called, and wanted to study further. My grandfather had pre-empted his daughters' need to learn and get a college or university degree and had written urgent letters to and agitated with the senior academics at a University (in northern India) to allow women to enter. My mother followed her sister to university and enrolled in Psychology and Logic (right brain and left-brain subjects) and told me that she enjoyed both. To ensure that his daughters did not feel isolated in 'college', my grandfather persuaded two of his friends to enrol their daughters in college study. I believe he was a man before his time – he showed he loved and cared for his daughters as much as he did his son – and would use his love of equality and liberalism to give them an education as well as persuading his friends to do the same for their daughters. My mother did well (passing subjects with distinction) till her third year when she met my father, a Royal Indian Air Force officer at a function, fell in love and lost (just for a little while) her abiding interest in learning and doing well academically.

I have always felt that my mother was a 'reincarnation' of Rani Padmini, a legendary fourteenth century Indian Hindu queen renowned for her beauty and courage. She seemed to have the Rani's spirit and looks and like the Rani, she was dedicated to her husband. As the ancient Indian legend goes, when the stories of her beauty came to the notice of the Muslim ruler of Delhi, he decided to attack Chittor to obtain her. He laid siege to the fort but Padmini's husband and his soldiers would not give in despite huge losses. The invader sent a message to the ruler, asking to see the beautiful queen. Initially the Raja refused saying that his wife along with other women of her status lived in seclusion in the women's quarters and could only be seen by men of their immediate family. After much persuasion, the Raja allowed the invading kind to see her in a mirror while she stood behind a screen. Seeing her beauty – out of reach - seems to have inflamed him further to win this beautiful woman. The siege continued till the fort of Chittor was almost taken at which time, the Raja rode out with his remaining soldiers for their last battle. All the soldiers died on the battle-field; however when the victorious invader entered the city, he discovered that the beautiful Rani and her female companions had committed *Johar* (immolating themselves in a fire) to protect their honour. The invader won the battle but lost the war!

My mother seemed to have been formed in the image of Rani Padmini – beautiful, wilful, fierce and deeply in love with her husband. She had flashing eyes, a beautiful face, one crooked ear, a hairstyle she was told made her look 'regal like Queen Victoria' and a brain which allowed her to succeed academically and verbally. I think my father was drawn to her flashing eyes and her good looks which reminded him of his favourite Indian movie star from the movie that he had watched nineteen times. She also had that deep vein of latent anger buried deep within her. Perhaps, unconsciously, she carried a rage similar to my paternal grandfather which may have drawn Dad to her. I don't think he had dealt with or worked through his resentment at the cruelty perpetrated on him by his father nor had he come to terms with what his father's rage was about. And like a child who plays with a match flame, putting his fingers in and out, he kept trying to reach the source or the wellspring of that anger.

Recently I read an article in a psychology magazine which commented that some couples loved the concept of fights akin to duelling amygdalas! They feel particularly challenged since our brains are wired for both attachment and self-protection. We want to be close to our partners and we also protect ourselves from pain by moving away through blame, withdrawal, and other ineffective coping strategies. When I read these comments I was struck by the fact that it described my parents perfectly.

Referring to the duelling amygdalas, my siblings particularly my brother and I experienced Mum's anger daily from a young age to the time we were twelve or thirteen years of age. Her anger was potent and latent, simmering close to the surface, and we felt it almost daily as children. It made her seem like a tigress or very like the black and rageful goddess Kali in my eyes. (In ancient Hindu paintings, Kali dances over her husband Shiva's body in joyful liberation but she also loves him just as I think my mother loved her children but would not take any impertinence from them.)

My mother had inherited a lot of her own mother's good looks and also a huge amount of her sadness (or this may have been subtly imbibed by her as she grew from a teenager to a young woman). When you read Kusum's mother's story, you will understand the nature of the trauma that haunted her. My grandmother had been stolen as a young girl from her family and fostered by a white missionary woman thousands of miles away from home. Grandma carried a deep sadness and a haunted look in her eyes. This is trans-generational trauma, which is often passed to the next and future generations through unconscious cues or psychic messages flowing between adults and children. Sometimes the anxiety transmits from one generation to the next through stories told. Sometimes an overwhelming and unnameable dread or sadness is passed on somatically to those who are close to us. Our loved ones often carry what we ourselves cannot.

In my mother's case, the sadness or intergenerational trauma took the form of anger and fear. She loved us but we also made her very angry, so she said. Her anger had its wellspring in the sadness she had witnessed in her mother, the stolen child. As psychology has shown, depression can sometimes be anger turned inwards. And sometimes it can be the other way around: sadness may be converted into anger – at the world, her lot in life (caring for her sick mother, waiting for her husband to return from his dangerous military work) and her wish to be free of earthly cares and woes. One of her greatest fears was to be a widow bringing up children on her own. She had everything in life that many Indian women would have wanted but she was probably a person who considered a glass half-empty and waited for some tragedy to strike. She could also have been affected by some form of PTSD (post-traumatic stress disorder) where hyper-vigilance and bouts of anger are common along with sadness and fear.

I was mortally afraid of my mother from six to twelve years of age when I experienced the worst of her fury. She would rain blows on us (her children) with sticks, rubber thongs, leather sandals and once with flatware from the dining table. To this day, I have nightmares about her fury. At times, when I am anxious or depressed, I talk to my therapist and when she asks 'how old are you?' I say 'seven, eight years old'. Those years live in my memory. She seemed to set supremely high standards and could not abide others not living by her standards. However, she was also fragile and wanted protection and care in many ways. She wanted to be loved by her husband to the exclusion of all others as well as by my grandfather, her father. She was the second daughter in the family and just as it happened I was the second child, second daughter in mine. My grandfather doted on his older daughter just as my mother and father doted on their oldest child, my older sister. However, she could never see the parallel when I stormed at her for playing favourites. I saw her throw severe tantrums in her grown-up years (when I was twelve or thirteen years old) when she discovered that her father had given his older daughter presents of gold jewellery for producing her one and only child something which she had never demanded nor expected when she had given birth to her own five children.

My mother told me years later that she had hated looking after her mother when she fell ill on her return from Europe with rheumatoid arthritis and was confined to her bed or a wheelchair. My mother was in her early teens when this happened and trauma at that life-stage can have strange and unforeseen effects. I also wondered why my grandmother fell ill? She had developed rheumatoid arthritis for which doctors then could not ascribe a cause.

I think, however, that her illness was related to abandonment and sadness issues that she had carried around with her from the death of her mother in infancy, being stolen as a young school-girl and being brought up thousands of miles away by a foster mother. Also, returning from Europe after three months and finding her children safe and well may well have been a relief but holding her will and resolve together to see them safe and happy may have metamorphosed into a new illness. She became fixed or fixated in her bones, never to leave her home again. This probably made sure that she stayed close to her children. I also think her illness turned into sadness, 'stuckness' and grief. A 'stolen child' who remained traumatised and pained to the very end.

I felt my mother was always ready to fight the good fight and sometimes when she was only mildly cross, it could escalate into the worst fight she could have. The slightest infraction whether it be a snappy remark or failure to immediately do as we were told or being woken from her afternoon nap roused her wrath and often brought out physical slaps, hits and punches along with verbal abuse such as 'I hope you rot in hell' and other harsh and damaging words. My brother and I experienced this as verbal and physical 'abuse' in the form of slaps, blows and harsh words, often being rescued by our nannies and sometimes by grandparents. I believe in her heart she may have meant well but she seemed to have dwelt in constant anxiety about her husband, his active risk-taking military role and moving from place to place as an army wife. Dark thoughts of a possible downfall from being a lady of high standing to being a widow with four or five children to support ate away at her. She could not brook the slightest challenge to her authority or anything which may rock her fragile standing as an upper-middle-class married woman with a family who could fall into poverty as a widow. In years to come, she would throw herself into religion - fundamental Christian religion, which promised an end to 'wickedness' and badness in the world and an idyllic happiness in the 'new' world to come.

Besides her fierce anger and high standards, she was also unashamedly vocal in her beliefs. She said she was a woman who loved truth and justice. She said she was unable to lie - she was officially off the list of people to ask when we were playing hide-and-seek with friends or family members because when asked 'have you seen so-and-so go past?' she would either smile or reply that she could not say. This implied that she had seen the person go past.

She was also a lonely woman though she was well-educated. She was a good conversationalist but she did not suffer fools gladly nor could she abide small talk. She found it hard to interact with women whose main topic of conversation was children's misbehaviours or cleverness, their little coffee parties, and minutiae of their gossip about their household staff. She needed conversation that was meaningful – of political, social and literary importance but did not get it from military wives. She would not go to tea and coffee parties calling them boring. She read books of all sorts and her bible and spent a lot of time reading us stories from the same.

As a child, I can remember my mother holding on to her Bible, always ready to turn to a Bible story of victory and annihilation. And some of my favourite close-to-Mom moments come from these times. She would often read out these stories to her three older children when we were marooned and alone in a new army cantonment far from her close family and few friends who lived in another city. I think it is this love of the Bible and its many 'inspiring' stories that sensitised her to wandering preachers and the promise of a world to come. As such she listened to missionaries and preachers who came by from time to time discussing doctrinal matters as well as the behaviour of followers who espoused the 'faith.'

My mother read a lot and I have inherited this love of books from her. I am reminded of her taste in bedtime stories apart from accounts from the Bible. Her tastes ranged from fairytales and moral fables for children, to ghost stories, factual adventure tales and interesting articles from newspapers which she read daily. I remember she read a book which dealt with the exploits of a hunter who tracked and killed man-eating tigers. She decided to read these stories to my siblings and I each night which enthralled us but frightened us so much that we would group together to go to bed.

Another one of her strange habits was reading and following the Indian Railway timetables. India has one of the largest railway networks in the world – courtesy of the British Raj. I didn't understand then what she got out of poring over time-tables – was she planning an escape from us or was she planning on how to escape and go to see our father when he was away for months on military exercises or just exercising her sharp brain to zigzag the country on adventurous holidays.

Initially, my mother and father (as people belonging to different religions – she a Christian and he from an orthodox Hindu family) had decided to be rational and reasonable and allow their children (the older three siblings) to go to various places of worship – temples to different Hindu gods or Sikh temples, churches of various denominations, as well as fundamentalist and little-known chapel groups, mosques, and so on. Whenever a friend came along and told them of a new place of worship, the three of us (we called ourselves the three musketeers) would be driven there the next week. There came a time I think when we did not know whether to sit, stand, sing or 'zombie' out when we went to a place of worship. I also think it was very confusing for children who were being asked to make up their own minds as to the nature of God, the universe, the nature of redemption and matters of religious doctrine. I do believe children need set values and beliefs early in life, allowing them to work out the actual ritual or religion they want to follow later. Later, my mother would fiercely decry the philosophy of various gurus and ecumenical leaders, which was prevalent at that time that 'all religions are true, and there is just one god. That we are all going to the same place; that many rivers lead to the ocean even if their paths never cross.'

My mother's need for redemption became a guiding force in her life. By the time I was seven or eight years old, she was entertaining travelling pastors and missionaries who found themselves at our door. She would be hospitable but she craved spiritual guidance and a way out of a world that she found unbearably sad and troubling. She took to heart all the scriptural exhortations and became convinced that if she were to follow all the Biblical commandments she may find a way into a better life. She became a devout member of a fundamentalist Christian church and took to studying the Bible frequently with us and exhorting us to do the same.

I have often wondered what attracted her to the fundamentalist religion she ultimately chose to follow. I think it was a combination of her need to believe, be redeemed and have the hope of a higher life. It may also have something to do with having set boundaries because ambiguity as posited by many eastern faiths did not appeal to her. It could also have been driven by her fierce desire to be good and god-loving and finding the narrow path that the normal world would not allow her to have. In a strange way, she was trying to find a concrete, fixed path to *nirvana* – a guarantee of a better life to come.

Recently I read a book on the attraction of religious fundamentalism and found some arguments which made sense to me as they seemed to have hooked into my mother's psyche. Fundamentalist religions seem to demand that the rationale for their beliefs be innovative in its own right; often times they say they have proof about the heresy of old established religions which seems incontrovertible. Many fundamentalist religions try to prove accepted orthodox religious dogma as wrong and misguided, based on myths and hoary old traditions. They want literalism and often insist that the old religions have moved away from the original tenets and foundations. Fundamentalism becomes a movement of conscious, organised opposition to disrupt the traditions and orthodoxies. In the end, they become the beleaguered martyrs holding on to the original tenets of Christianity and being persecuted by the old orthodox religions.

Like my mother, fundamentalists are not comfortable with the culture of their times. She looked for a conscious and conscientious vindication of her faith and it became her badge of separation from the world. She relished and gloried in it and was soon teaching and inculcating it in us as children. Soon my siblings and I were baptised in this faith and taught to spread this faith. Weekly, we were sent to roam the narrow alleys of cities knocking on doors and preaching to people who wondered open-mouthed who we were. Posh, educated and well-dressed teenagers who were often dropped in a chauffeur-driven car near the street where we had to preach our message of faith. Yes, the juxtaposition of wandering around preaching God's message in the midst of this poverty and the personal wealth we came from was not lost on us. I think people we met and talked to were both bemused and confused, perhaps taken aback at this strange religion we were bringing to them.

While my mother had the values of a saint, likely inculcated by her parents and her readings of the Bible, she had the imperious temper of a *maharani* deprived of her jewels. Being without a mother for three crucial months of her teenage growing years and later watching her mother go from an acute illness of rheumatoid arthritis to a chronically and deeply ill woman, crippled and confined to her bed, broke her inner resolve to be a gracious and stately lady. I believe she lived in psychological fear for the rest of her life - always on the edge of disbelief and fear that she would lose her social privileges, high-living lifestyle, handsome and ambitious military husband, any modicum of wealth and any number of things that could possibly go wrong in any human's life.

She followed Dad to various military stations (or cantonments) where there was a severe lack of facilities including schools good enough for her children. Dad, however, loved his military life – being at the Officers Mess, taking parades, steeped in artillery or parachuting lore, playing cards with his friends at the Club, camaraderie with brother officers were the stuff that my mother 'hated'. She hated living on military bases which did not offer her the wide variety of experiences and people to communicate with nor the anonymity to follow her own interests, things that she craved. She did not want the trappings of being an army wife particularly of a man who was going up the military ladder. She was an independent thinker and a highbrow intellectual, who looked down on people who lived the hedonistic and 'low' life of cards, parties, gossip and army ceremonies. She was also a lonely woman because though she was well-educated and a good conversationalist she did not suffer fools gladly. In many ways, she was shy and introverted; she was always stiff and stood apart from other army wives and would often beg Dad before they went out not to leave her to the mercies of the army wives. She said she could not stand their endless stories of their mah-jong and card games and 'kitty' parties or recounting the minutiae of what their maid-servants and children did on a daily basis. She found such talk boring and said she needed conversation that was rational and meaningful – of political, social and literary importance which she did not get it from military wives. She wanted conversation on politics, social and current affairs issues with men whom she found more down-to-earth and not as shallow as their wives. I thought she was odd then but now I empathise with her and understand her point of view and refrain from friendships which are simply *coffee-klatches*, where a group of women sit and chatter about who did what where.

My mother was to have two more children – a daughter who was ten years younger than I and a son who was seventeen years younger. After her initial shock, she got used to the idea of her third daughter, who was to become the mainstay of her life and often took the role of a close friend. But she could not get over having a child when she was forty, just when she was beginning to feel free of children and looking after a household. My youngest brother felt the brunt of her persistent anger from an early age. Considered bipolar, he encapsulated the psychological belief that the most sensitive member of the family is the bearer of the sadness, anger and other dysfunctions in the family. He was truly the lost child.

Some years later, just after my maternal grandfather died, my parents, at the urging of my older sister, went to live in USA. My parents left behind the grand homes and lifestyle that they had enjoyed. Partly, they knew they were growing older and needed to be near family who could look after them. They wanted my younger sister, then twenty-one, to marry a suitable man and have a better life and also believed they needed help with my younger brother. They were in their mid- to late-fifties and had to start life all over again in another country. India to USA was as far as the Earth is from Mars. But the same spirit which caused my mother to learn and adapt was to stand her in good stead. She learnt to drive managing to obtain a driving licence after six failed attempts. It was a real laugh to see my parents own two old junk cars. This was because each of them had to have their own car even if it was just to drive to the supermarket or the drycleaners – but those old cars were spotlessly kept and maintained.

Both were great adapters and found themselves thriving after their initial bouts of homesickness subsided. They learnt to live frugally. Both of them learnt to absorb themselves in the society where they lived – a far cry from their up-scale life with family retainers and a vibrant social circle in India.

Mum also learned to absorb herself into a new culture on the west coast of USA and kept up her learning and adapting herself to the changing mores till she was well into old age. She had decided to cast aside her saris (except on very formal occasions) and strode around in pant-suits, even taking up shorts in summer. She made friends with white, black and Hispanic people and kept herself up-to-date with news and current affairs.

I felt sad and angry when I saw my mother being condescended and talked down to in this western country in the latter quarter of the twentieth century. I often wondered how people could patronise (a subtle form of racism and discrimination) a woman who had a Bachelors degree in Psychology, which she had studied and received in the early 1940's, who had lived an upper-class lifestyle all her life, married a man of means, run a household of six to eight household staff, gone places in a chauffeur-driven car, and never done a day of paid work in her life. Did they see in her a poor Indian woman standing outside her hovel waiting for a dollar from some kind passer-by? Did they feel they had to educate, instruct and guide her around because though lived in another country she spoke their language with class and had a fine education?

As I have noted earlier, inherent racism and currents of superiority was present in articles published by various magazines right up to the nineteen sixties. Such magazines portrayed people in African and south Asian countries as poor natives, sometimes labourers or exotics, frequently unclothed, chopping wood or collecting firewood, living amidst nature and akin to natural animals – a kind of noble savage. Never did they portray people in various parts of Africa or the Indian sub-continent as educated people with large houses, cars, means of support and going about in occupations similar to their white cousins in another country.

As my parents got older, my mother's health began to deteriorate. This was evident once Dad died at the age of eighty-eight. My mother despite a live-in housekeeper-companion and then going into a nursing home started sliding into dementia when she was eighty plus years of age and dying aged eighty-eight years. Despite her dementia, some things stuck in her brain. Once while visiting her in her nursing home, I walked in and sat down by her side and took her hand. She looked at me quizzically and I could see she felt she ought to know me. With a straight face, I told her I was her sixth child whom she had abandoned in India thirty-five years before. Her face twisted in horror and rage. She yelled at me: 'I have never abandoned any child. I have had five children and proceeded to name each one of us in the right order'. Shamefaced, I apologised and acknowledged that I had been playing with her. It took a while for her to calm down.

I did learn many things consciously and unconsciously from my mother. One was her love of learning and being educated. I can remember that whenever we moved and set up home, she would put a desk in a corner of a room and this was dedicated to her reading and writing. She spent a lot of time in religious works but she also loved current affairs and political discourse.

She particularly loved logic which she had studied at college and she loved to disprove people who were superstitious or illogical in putting forth premises for discussion. She called herself an 'iconoclast' and would deliberately walk under ladders or step on cracks in the pavement to prove that superstition was not to going to stop her from leading an open and courageous life.

She was also quite irreverent and disparaging of nationalism which she believed divided peoples of one land or internationally. Many a time to Dad's horror, she refused to stand for national anthems or put hand on heart to take pledges of allegiance because her first allegiance was to God. She also insisted that she was always truthful and her word was her bond and she would tell you the truth without taking any oaths and pledges.

When asked the questions - Which of your parents are you most like and why, I know I am more like my father than my mother though I do carry many of her qualities. I don't believe I have her angry traits. I am more stoic in my behaviour; I try to combine logic and reason (that she liked and used) with compassion and lack of judgement. Is this because I have disavowed religion and have undertaken a lot of personal therapy in my aim at 'differentiation' and individuation?

At the same time, I am like her in many ways. I believe I have inherited many of her good social values and have also chosen the harder path or the road less travelled. However, there is at least one aspect where I differ markedly from her. I am an avowed feminist and have left the religion instilled in me by my mother because I could not stand patriarchal men - uneducated, unversed, unskilled, lacking compassion - tell me how to run my life. I could not also take the exhortations of men from the pulpit because they said it was God's purpose for women and men. I found enough biblical grounds to let my mother and those of my family who are still ingrained in their religion know that god did not put inequality in people's hearts. What was perhaps traditional and perhaps fitting two thousand years ago when the bible was written was not to be used literally today.

I have found a different spirituality. I have discovered the power of love and empathy for the ones who need my care and comfort; I have found it easy to take up the cudgels for people who do not have the skills or expertise. I believe in working against violence of all sorts (domestic, economic, political, emotional) And I found a man, a life partner, who made his way into my heart when I first met him with similar beliefs. In our first or second meeting when discussing a subject we were interested in, I said 'Who knows? Only god knows!' And to my delighted surprise he said 'Whatever She says!' I was amazed at this reply and when I asked if he thought god was a woman, he said he did not know whether god was male or female but kept an open mind about it.

I wish more people had these views. My mother for all her feistiness, intelligence, education and knowledge eventually submitted herself to the control of (religious) men and their thinking. She was not prepared to declare 'this is what I think' living to the end of her life faithful to the idea of being a subservient god-fearing woman.

MY GRANDMOTHER –
WHITE LILY OF PEACE

My maternal grandmother was given a Tamil name by her parents, which meant 'the lucky one', and later a Biblical name by her foster mother. She was filled with kindness and mercy for all whom she saw though she could not find enough of this quality to heal herself. She was a 'stolen' child and her life was full of pain and sorrow for the life and parents she had lost as a child. The veneer of Christianity sat on her like a flowing robe but her heart was like a rich merchant on the banks of mother river Ganges who gave out the alms of love and compassion, hoping for nirvana and spiritual riches in another life. She gave to others the love and care she had craved as a child. I believe she did not keep any love and compassion for herself. I think she would become burnt out because of the amount of care and compassion she gave away. I often think of her as a modern-day Mirabai, that beautiful poet-saint who had lived in fifteenth century in India. Despite pressure from her family, legend tells us that the widowed Mirabai refused to immolate herself on her husband's funeral pyre, preferring a life of spirituality and dedication to her god.

My grandmother, in any age and time, would be considered a remarkable woman. She was an independent thinker, resolute in her beliefs, compassionate, mindful of the hurts and anxieties of others but personally stoic and somehow removed from her own sadness and pain.

She was born into a prosperous, middle-class south Indian family from the trader caste, around the turn of the twentieth century likely 1900. She was among the first women of her family and likely society to study at an English school. Her name which meant 'fortune favours her' or 'the lucky one', perhaps embodied her parents' wishes for her. She was the youngest daughter in a family of three sisters and a brother. Her mother had died giving birth to her and their father had married again and brought a stepmother into their home. The 'lucky one' was still a baby and clung to her sisters perhaps thinking of them as substitutes for her lost mother. She craved love and attention for herself but had to act grown up - she had to help in cooking and cleaning the house and caring for her new stepbrother. Her father was canny and ambitious; he was a building developer, undertaking ambitious projects for British colonial councils, as well as various rulers and rajahs. His work included building large civil offices for the town council and a palace for a Rajah (both buildings stand today). However, according to my grandmother, her merchant-builder father was not a moral human being; he was mean-spirited and cheated the poor workers, who slaved for a few coins a day. He would review each day's work and find many faults for which he would deduct workers' wages as he saw fit. The men who had spent all day hauling stones and laying bricks or carving traditional statues in rooms or verandas surrounding the palace would go away with less than enough to feed their families. Many a time, my grandmother and her sisters heard workers curse their father for his meanness and miserliness. Later in life, she came to believe that those curses had affected her health and wellbeing, because ill-wishes of poor neglected people do not go away but come home to roost!

This child who loved knowledge and learning, like her two older sisters, was sent by her upwardly mobile, 'enlightened' father to an English-speaking school run by Christian missionaries. Such was the reach of these English-teaching schools that the girls sent there were attributed to have the manners and knowledge of white 'memsahebs' and yet be untouched or soiled by uncouth youths. This would also lead to their getting good husbands on the marriage market due to their learning and good manners. This would be in addition to their upbringing, the domestic skills learnt from their mothers, and the big dowries that would be attached to them. The missionaries knowing the apparent advantages attached to the girls in their school took advantage of the situation to 'brainwash' them with Christian ideas. The girls were told that all religion such as Hindu, Muslim and all others apart from Christianity were false, full of idols and unknown rituals, the arena of the ignorant and 'damned'. Religious instruction or Bible-classes were mandatory and the regular indoctrinations soon hit the mark. Instead of gods and goddesses with many arms and heads, the girls learnt about the sweet and humble Jesus and his aim to attract people of all sorts to him. All who came to him would be saved, no matter what they had done, just as long as they believed. They would not need to go through a million lives of incarnation to finally get redemption or 'nirvana'. My grandmother told me that this was a stark revelation to her sisters and herself. No more having to come back as a cockroach or an ant or a worm; no more reincarnations to come back to better stations and caste positions in society; no more endless denials of one's self. Believe in Jesus and you will go straight to heaven. Such simplicity of access, such removal of obfuscation, such easy attainment of ultimate bliss.

Within a year, the oldest sister was talking of converting to Christianity but knowing her father planned to marry her to a rich suitor soon, she asked the missionaries for help. 'I want to be a good Christian girl, but my father won't let me', she cried. 'He will kill me and my sisters.' She was not far wrong since Christianity till then was reserved for the people from the lower castes, those at the bottom of the ladder, who were downtrodden and shunned by people of the castes above them. Such lower caste Indians and untouchables including converts lived outside the villages, did not draw water from the same well nor did their shadow fall across higher caste Indians. Many of the lower caste Indians had taken advantage of the food and education given out by the white missionaries and been baptised and were often referred to as the 'rice Christians'. Having read some narratives and talked to some in my youth I understand a few said that baptism was just another bath in the river and did not mean anything more than that - as long as it brought them food, housing and education.

Their older sister's dilemma soon spread to the younger ones. She had been their second mother, the one who had looked after them when their own mother died. Their stepmother was not cruel, just indifferent. A year after marrying their father she had given birth to a son, who had become the light of the parents' eyes. Soon, the sisters were going to school with pent breaths and heavy hearts wondering when their father would find out about their beliefs in Christianity and lock them, thus preventing them from going to school. Their world had opened up and now it would close up again like thunder and lightning which stopped picnics and walks in the park.

The youngest, the lucky one as her name implied, began to look for signs of good luck. One night, she saw Halley's Comet for the first time. Her father, stepmother, older sisters and neighbours watched the night skies and began to whisper that this would be an evil year for the country and indeed, for the British Empire, their colonial masters. Some began to hope that Indians would rebel for a second time against the empire and establish nationhood for themselves. Night after night, the comet came across the sky as the 'lucky one' watched with her family. She was convinced that this carried bad news for their sister's escape and their own abandonment. Soon, they clamoured 'Whatever is good enough for our older sister is good enough for us. We want to become Christians too.' The missionaries' work was now complete.

The comet was still streaking across the sky when they went to school one day. My grandmother was probably eight or nine years old but she was clever and knew how to keep her own counsel. She had overheard the teacher-missionaries discussing 'the plan' the day before at school – which was to whisk the girls away by train to a small mission in northern Indian (approx. 1500 miles away) run by Christian missionaries. They would be safe - the girls would live with others in a dormitory and finish their education, later to become teachers or nurses. And that's what eventually happened. One day the girls did not come home from school. Their father raced around the neighbourhood enquiring about the girls' whereabouts. He then went to the school after it had closed for the day to ask whether the girls had been delayed with homework or gone somewhere on a picnic. The answer was that they had gone far away. Apparently, he screamed and yelled, in torment, and soon the neighbourhood was up in arms. A citizens' riot took place. The police were called to manage the situation but the police (under British rule) were on the side of the missionaries and refused to help him. His girls were lost and so was he! He did not realise how much he had loved them and all that is known is that it broke his heart. He continued to run his business without his former zest, leaving it to his son to grow up and take over operating the business. The son was never to be as clever or as mean as his father. Soon the family business disappeared from view and from the rich commerce of the city.

The 'lucky one' travelled with her sisters for days before she arrived at a small village in the Punjab. She did not understand their language but she knew English. Her days were haunted by images and memories of her father and brother; she sometimes also thought of her baby half-brother. She was sad because there was no one now to spoil her, wash her hair and oil it, then put fragrant flowers in her hair, make her favourite food of rice and vegetable curry or talk lovingly to her. The old days had gone. Her older sister now worked part-time as a teacher's assistant to defray her boarding costs and the two younger ones lived in a dormitory, eating what was given them and working hard at their studies. They knew no one in the neighbourhood and no one played with these strange girls who did not talk the local language. They started going to the local school run by missionaries of the Christian mission and soon the cleverness of the two younger girls was evident. They were excellent in English and Mathematics and 'the lucky one' became proficient in embroidery and sewing. She was small as a bird and quiet but underneath there was a strong and resolute heart. One of the missionaries at the mission which ran the school and its dormitory took a liking to her and decided to adopt her. The missionary mother changed the lucky one's name to Hope. This was an apt choice for a little 'lost' girl, torn from her parents, whose hope for love and kindness had brought her to her current state and would colour her nature for the rest of her life. She was also a spiritual person and would pour out loving care and compassion for all that she came across. However, no one ever bothered to ask Hope if she was happy... did she miss her father... did she miss the life she had in the southern city she had come from? And Hope did not put up her hand and complain to anyone. She absorbed it all; she internalised her pain and sadness and showed her brave face to the world. Her stoic nature was both a quality of Indian women as well as a feature of the internalisation of pain that she practiced for the rest of her life. That stoicism would become a stream of experience in her family going through her daughter and to her grand-daughter (myself).

I have heard that anger becomes sadness when turned inward. Hope was young and sad. Hope's depression was to do with her young life which had been turned upside down because of following her sister and the sister's love of Christianity. But to complain would mean that her older sister would be distressed for turning her youngest sister's life upside down and that would make it one vast cloud of sadness.

So she stuffed the unhappiness down into herself and set about learning all she could of Christianity and its beliefs, its scriptures and to practice it like no one had ever practiced it before. She became a saint par excellence! Her studies and knowledge of Christianity would be conflated with her own private value system of courage, justice and conscience. She resolved to always speak her truth but to do so compassionately and with grace and kindness.

Her adoptive mother also fostered a few other girls particularly those who lived in the dormitories and had nowhere to go when school closed for the summer vacation. Hope made friends with one of the other girls a good natured but scatty young woman who loved to giggle and read romances. They became friends though Hope's innate introversion and incipient sadness would not allow her to spend time giggling and laughing or sharing stories about young men that they fancied. She was Miss Sober herself! She worked on her books and studies, helped her adoptive mother with household chores and took a keen interest in all things Christian and church-related! She would never lose this interest and keep it to the end of her life. Her Bible was well-thumbed and marked, she had exercise books full of scriptures and notes on whom to talk to and visit with a jar of chutney or jam and a kind word.

One of the stories she told me of her childhood remain with me. Hope had an adoptive younger sister, called Mala, who was not into good works. She loved young men with oiled hair and grins on their faces, who promised to take her to the movies or behind the church hall for a quick kiss after Sunday church. Mala was a 'normal' young woman in her prime and she enjoyed these little excursions into love and liberty intensely. One night, she came to see Hope and sat on the edge of her bed and talked till it was past midnight. Hope wanted her sleep but she also liked her friend and did not want to cause a rift with Mala by asking her to go away and let her sleep. It was the height of summer and the girls slept on light stretcher beds with cotton sheets and bedding on the back veranda. Screens kept out the worst of the mosquitoes. Mala and Hope went out to get a drink of water from the large round earthenware water vessel kept on the steps outside the veranda. Hope got her cup of water first and went back to bed to sleep. As she fell asleep, she heard Mala cry out and thought it was one of her young suitors who had turned up for a midnight tryst and turned over to sleep. An hour later, their mother went out to get some water and saw Mala lying by the veranda steps. She shone a torch around to discover what had happened and saw a huge cobra wrapped around the earthen vessel - the coolest place for this venomous snake. Apparently, the cobra had struck Mala as she got her cup of water. Hope would never forget her own close brush with death, was ever watchful of snakes and would mourn Mala and her untimely death for many years.

Fifteen years later, Hope would discover a *krait* (one of India's deadliest snakes) lying in a crack on a side veranda of the house she shared with her husband and their three children. And twenty years after the krait's appearance and removal, she would whisper to me to call Grandpa because she saw a snake climbing a creeper on the front veranda where we were sitting. She was recounting bed-time stories to us, her grand-daughters. Was she hyper-alert to the presence of snakes in her native land? Or was her unconscious alerting her to snakes or underhanded people who surrounded her at all times?

As World War I ended, my remarkable grandmother went on to study medicine. She wanted to heal people and help them to be well and healthy again. Her adoptive mother arranged for her to go to a medical school close by even though women did not study much further than a few classes of primary school if they were lucky. She worked through two years of medicine before she came home for the holidays and met a young man called Aaron, who had just returned from World War I where he had served as a Chaplain and Welfare Officer in the Middle East with the forces of the British empire. He too wanted to help the poor and be of service to others. He was to join the YMCA (Young Men's Christian Association) and devote his life to helping and assisting the poor and needy. Their partnership seemed to have been 'made in heaven' as they say. Her adoptive mother persuaded her to marry Aaron who was a fine young man according to her and told Hope that they could do much good with their lives. So Hope left her studies at medical school but never gave up on her goal to help people in her community. It was to start her on her role in being active in social and community work.

She was a woman who would always speak her mind doing so with respect and firmness. Once when sitting with a group of women who were meeting with the Bishop's wife, she heard them 'gossip' about a woman whom they felt was having an affair with a fellow parishioner. The women in her group, as they sat sipping tea and nibbling on cakes and sandwiches, were determined to teach this woman a lesson. They decided they would stop talking to her; they would shun her and teach her how decent women behaved. The Bishop's wife as she took tea with the women went along with the groupthink. Hope sat and listened quietly for a while until she could take no more and spoke out: 'How will this woman know what is the right thing to do? Surely, we ought to draw her close and show her how decent women behave?' Shocked silence ensued. The Bishop's wife got the point. And the women in the group got the point. Perhaps all the women were so engaged in their personal vendettas as well as their enjoyment of salacious tales that they forgot who they were. That's what Hope thought.

Hope had thought that Aaron's family seemed to love her because they had accepted her into their large clan but she often heard

Aaron's younger brothers make fun of people from southern India and their accent when speaking Hindi and their culinary love of what they called 'pepper-water'. Hope had tolerated their thoughtless jokes for some years until they started joking and poking fun behind the back of the local accountant who was a South Indian man. This time, Hope's values and forthrightness came to the fore and she confronted them, pointing out their bad manners in making fun of South Indians when she herself was one and they were enjoying her hospitality! Embarrassed, they mumbled into their tea and changed the subject, never to do it again in her hearing.

One day, Aaron who had been a Welfare & Personnel Officer with a large industrial group owned by British interests and who had used ingenious ways to help working men and women working in such factories, such as schools for children and crèches for the young, gyms for young men and women, rehabilitation by learning new crafts and arts for injured workers, received a letter through the YMCA and the British-German Friendship League, of which he was a member. (Note: the British-German League would not be dismantled till later in the decade when Hitler's true intentions were unmasked.) The invitation said that he and his wife were invited to come to England and Germany and visit other nations in Europe to see for themselves how the European people work for progress and achieving the common goal of peace and security.

Aaron was thrilled to receive such a letter. He went home to Hope and discussed it with her. At dinner, he said: 'We should go because I believe we can learn more about how modern countries are progressing in helping people to lead better lives and achieve progress'. His daughters and son were enthralled because no one they knew had left India to go on a visit to England or Germany or indeed any other country. Only the very rich or people from the ruling class Rajahs and Ranis went to England or Europe. They demanded:

"What will you bring back for us? How will you get there? Who will stay with us when you are gone?" The discussion raged for days. Hope was hesitant because she cared deeply for her children and their wellbeing. Her daughters were going to an English school for girls – and her son was in an elite primary school. "We will see" she kept saying while her husband and children demanded she make up her mind.

Hope had grown up with an adoptive missionary mother from age ten onwards but in reality she was a 'stolen' child. She could not forget her father and the life she had growing up in a large family. She was still traumatised about losing her father, societal culture and her status as a wealthy Hindu girl. Losing family or even sight of her family for a few months reminded her of her own pain. The thought of her children being in a boarding school and having the school principal as their guardian, as was proposed, struck a raw chord in her heart. The sadness of her first few years in a faraway school in a faraway city, followed by years of wanting to belong still haunted her. She was paralysed by fear of something happening to her, never seeing them again. She felt she could not deal with the loss of not seeing her children daily for three or four months or knowing her children were being looked after by strangers. (Did my mother remember this fear transmitted by her own mother and always refuse to let us – her children – go to boarding school?) Hope wanted to cling to them and keep them close but she also wanted to know more about working in communities using new and innovative ideas.

Pushed and urged by her husband and friends, she finally went to the principal of her daughters' school and enquired if something could be done to solve her problem. The Principal liked Hope and her kindly ways so she offered to have the children stay with her in her home while the parents were away for three months travelling and visiting Europe. Hope was still unhappy because she had never left her children alone for a day or even a week let alone three months! She walked around in the garden of her home they called Heart's Delight praying for a solution. Aaron loved his children but he was confident that all would be well and that they should go to Europe. Finally, she gave her consent to the three-month journey of travel and visiting England, France, Switzerland and Germany. They travelled to Mumbai, got on a large ship and travelled via the Suez to Southampton. It was a long and arduous journey and Hope was dreadfully sick for weeks with nausea and food poisoning before she found her sea-legs.

Soon they were in London meeting with various luminaries of the YMCA Council. They would journey to Geneva to meet members of the founding committee and from there to Paris and to Berlin, Hamburg and Frankfurt. These were exciting times as Aaron and Hope met with Europeans who were fascinated by the Indian YMCA member, Aaron, and his beautiful Indian wife. This was Aaron's show and Hope played the part of the self-effacing Indian woman who would stay in the background and allow Aaron to meet and greet the towering figures of the organisation whom he so admired. She wrapped herself in her silk saris and held the *pallu* (last yard of the sari) over her head like a true, follower-wife. The men talked of the need for service, to lift up the downtrodden poor and bringing in practical programs to help the factory-workers and their families. Hope stayed in the background, talking to the wives of the officials, engaging in tea-parties and left the women gasping because of her lovely society manners, her grasp of the English language and her deep value systems about social work and community help. However, in her heart, she yearned for practical ways of serving others. Her heart felt the deep isolation and loss of her young children – she fell into re-experiencing her lost childhood with many elements of trauma – loss, hyper-alertness, sadness, searching for the lost other, all coming to the fore. Aaron did notice occasionally that she seemed lost in another world or in a dream-like state but he was too busy being a man, perhaps not too much in contact with his inner feelings and very much an Anglophile to realise that he was being patronised and brought into line as a subject of British Empire.

They went to Paris – taking in the sights of the Eiffel Tower, Notre Dame and then Versailles. Elegant Hope wanted to visit the Rue du Faubourg and Rue St. Honore and she got to do so, absorbing the beauty, style and culture. She wrote long letters and postcards to her children which would travel by boat arriving just before she returned. But writing helped her to stay in touch with her children, whom she felt she had deserted just in the same manner as she had been as a young girl. She bought little gifts for her lively daughters and the son whom she protected and adored. Men and women on the streets of Paris stared at this elegant woman as she walked around with her new women friends who chattered to her in French which she barely understood. Some thought of her as a Maharani, which she was not. Hope's heritage was from the middle-class or the merchant caste though they had accumulated wealth. Her adoptive mother was a missionary so she did not know much of how the aristocracy behaved except the elegance and grace she had absorbed, which was in her heart and her bones.

Wherever she travelled to in Europe, she was adulated and feted by the officials and their wives as they met and greeted her and Aaron. Outwardly she seemed happy but she fretted for her children, convinced that her desertion would affect them as it had affected her when she lost touch with her own father and family as a little girl. She believed her children would carry the mark of isolation, sadness and despair. She also fretted about the curses the workmen had heaped on her own builder-father and that it would affect her and future generations. The many layers of sadness seemed to have piled up in her life. Her only living family was her older sister; her middle sister having died at age twelve in their faraway school in the north, just before Hope was adopted by her missionary mother.

Finally, Hope and Aaron reached Berlin. Aaron had long admired the Germans as orderly, clean, detail-minded and upright. Soon they were surrounded by men in brown shirts and black shirts with swastikas on their armbands giving them detailed itineraries of what they would see and do in the fortnight they would spend in Germany. Large cars ferried them about as they went from factory to factory, offices, social camps, and hospitals. Aaron was deeply impressed as it melded with his belief that the Germans were well organised, highly moral people and were making it a better world for their own people. Aaron, as an Anglophile, subscribed to the belief that the two countries together with their complementary ideals would make it a better world or society for the emerging populations of the world. According to historical books, Britain and Germany had formed a special organisation in 1935 called the Anglo-German Fellowship comprised of influential members of British and German society including business people and diplomats. Apparently, the aim was not to make Britain a Nazi nation but to strengthen links between the two countries by hosting grand dinners and events where Anglophiles or Germanophiles such as prominent members of the aristocracy on the British side and political and industrial leaders on the German side were patrons and guests of honour.

The couple went on a visit to an industrial or social camp in Germany as arranged by their hosts. As they passed under the high arch leading into the large courtyard of the work camp, Hope saw the words 'Arbeit macht frei' in large wrought-iron letters above the camp gates. She asked what it meant and was told of their significance and meaning. Work can make you free. Strange words, she thought. Can work really make you free? The labourers and workers back in India would toil all day and seemed more like slaves not free men she thought. As they walked through the manufacturing facility-cum-work camp, where a few people toiled she shivered. She thought the place was dark and gloomy, with long corridors leading off in all directions and little rooms with very few windows leading off the corridors.

This was not like the sunshine and light of the India that she came from. She looked keenly at the men striding around with fervour and a sense of direction. They look earnest, she thought, full of patriotism and an ideal of making their country great or greater still. One of the officials approached her and talked to her about his country's friendship with Indians and some great Indian leaders. The men who met Hope felt that India was a great country full of great mineral wealth and other riches and any ties with Germany would help both countries. There seemed to be a sort of latent anxiety to impress this Indian couple so that they could spread the word about the friendly and helpful Germans when they returned home.

Aaron was mightily impressed. In their first night at the hotel where they stayed, he talked earnestly and enthusiastically of all he had observed in Germany, in their factories and their streets. India needs to be like this, said Aaron, who hated germs, dirt and disease. Hope smiled quietly as she heard Aaron glow with words but she felt a deep unease that things could not be that wonderful. She wanted to bring Aaron's great and glowing ideas and ideology down to reality. After hearing him for a while, she said: "I wonder what's behind all their earnestness and their wonderful goodwill? What's behind their love of sanitation and hatred of germs and fear of anyone who could be germ-ridden? I know you like all the cleanliness but I wonder what they are trying to whitewash." Aaron was startled by her words and acted as if he had been shot. He replied grimly "Trust you to not trust anyone". Hope knew this to be true. She found it hard to trust everyone - not after she have been deceived by various people and later discovered their motives – for example by her teachers, who later whisked her and her sisters away to make them Christians. But Aaron, a second-generation Christian man was an Anglophile, a Europhile and definitely a Germanophile. He was also a *germophobe* and a lover of all things organised and clean. He was to maintain this love and admiration for all things German and European all his life. So he remained enthralled and impressed.

The next day, Aaron had forgotten Hope's acerbic and suspicious comments. Their hosts picked them up after breakfast and they went to visit yet another dreary work camp-cum-social endeavour several miles in another direction. This time besides the endless corridors and little rooms, there were dormitories, kitchens, dining rooms and a couple of watchtowers near the entrance with the same words above the entrance *'Arbeit macht frei'*. All was clean but dreadfully spartan. There were officials around but not many people actually in the factory area. Perhaps they were out for the day, foraging or collecting material, thought Hope. Aaron was nervous around Hope, hoping she would not give voice to her concerns and thus annoy their hosts. He stole quick glances at her and often put his arm around her shoulders so as to comfort her or so Hope felt. Hope smiled her secret smile and kept her resolve not to pull his leg. She spoke graciously and asked questions about the kitchens and dining rooms and house-keeping issues, as if she were a normal *hausfrau* not the mistress of several household staff in her home in India.

No smile split her face as they walked around silently in the spacious yard in front of the building. As they went around the corner, she saw a sea of cornflowers, blue heads nodding in the wind. She exclaimed with delight: "Look, look, how beautiful they are! This reminds me of my home with its flowers and the lily pond full of hyacinths floating on the water!" As they say flowers bloom in swamps!

The group of men broke into smiles. Two of the officials came over and started gathering an armful of flowers for the lovely Frau Hope. Aaron, happy to have the ice broken, joined in and soon they had a huge bunch of blue cornflowers for Hope. Peace and calm was restored. The head official (the one with the polished boots and swastika on his armband) relaxed and whispered *'Gut, Gut, Frau Hope. Du bist eine schoene Inderinen.'* (Good, Mrs. Hope. You are a beautiful Indian woman)

Two years after they returned home from Europe, word began to spread about the horrors of *Kristallnacht* (Nov.1938) and then another two or three years as World War II raged the whispers became loud calls and news of the woes and murderous cleansing happening in Germany. Aaron was shocked and furious beyond words. "I could kick myself" he said to Hope. "I loved Germany and its cleanliness and organisation, meeting people of like mind and ideals, people devoted to serving humanity. I thought they wanted the best of all their people but they really fooled me. I thought they were like me raising public funds and putting in their own money to house workers, build community centres, schools and crèches for factory women and their children. I really thought the wonderful Germans were doing the same for all their people. Now when I read of their crimes and the purges, the way they have rounded up Jews, like the Silvers living up the street and who have done nothing to deserve it, I am really angry."

Hope replied "That was so deceitful of them. So shocking and heart-breaking. I honestly felt at that time that it was too good to be true. It seemed as if they were hiding something. And so they were. It should not have been named 'Work makes you Free' but 'Slave till you die'". Tears rolled down her face and Aaron joined her in her sadness.

The trauma and the deception affected them deeply because she had made service to the poor, the sick and needy her life's work apart from looking after her family. Aaron had supported her in her community activities not only because they complemented his own role of service as a Welfare & Personnel Officer but both had the attitude of serving others firmly in their hearts. It bound them in their life's resolve. Hope was often to be seen around the town they lived in either in a horse and carriage they kept (with a carriage-driver) or in her husband's car and had also taken to riding on her own on a bicycle wrapped in an elegant sari.

Soon after World War II ended, Aaron raced around their home picking up albums of photographs, framed photographs, souvenirs such as traditional porcelain figurines and bottles of cologne plus any other books, postcards or knick-knacks they had brought back from Germany. He tore the photographs into pieces, broke the figurines and hurled them all into a bin. And the bottles of cologne went straight down the toilet. He could not stand it. He thought: 'How dare they deceive us? Because they thought we were little brown men and women from a far away land? My heart feels sick when I think of my Jewish and wonderful Christian friends in Vienna and Berlin and Paris. They enslaved them in those camps which said Work makes you free, they killed them. He decided to get rid of those awful memories'.

Two photographs of a work camp and two newspaper cuttings were to survive - saved by their older daughter, my aunt, to see the light of day thirty years later. My mother, siblings and I would muse over them and try to find meaning in their historical relevance and the perversion of justice and humanity.

My grandparents were explicit and conjoint in their belief. They felt they had been duped. Their thoughts ran along the lines of: 'the

Nazis thought we were little brown men and women and would never find out about their perversions and the hatred that was directed at us. They patronised us. They kept us like puppy dogs on a leash, showing us the white-washed lies of their inhumanity. And we were like lambs, led to the altar of their lies and the slaughter of the innocence of millions of humans. The officials wore the *swastika* but they were the wrong way around. Still the word (coming from Sanskrit) meant something that was *'genuine' and 'pure'*. It wasn't pure or innocent or just in any way. We sacrificed the health of our filial relationships and the goodwill of friends to spend months being fed lies'.

Hope, the stolen child, went through another experience of having her innocence stolen from her yet again. The child who marvelled at Hailey's comet, who went to school to learn English and some of the great values as taught by the missionaries was to be robbed of her innocence and beliefs in white men's teachings yet again. She, who had been taken away in the name of Christianity and humanity and torn from her father and family, now lost faith in white people's ability to give her the truth. Was she to experience yet again the 'shell' game? The puzzle, wrapped in a mystery, and re-wrapped in an enigma? The 'lucky one', the woman who had lost her youth when she was torn from her natural family at age eight or nine, losing the sister closest to her in age to death when Hope was only eleven or twelve, was unlucky yet again. Her life was a cup of sadness that kept being re-filled by life and the circumstances she endured. Very likely the loss of her father and family and the girls' rude and sudden transportation to a distant place drew illness and ill-health to her.

Her oldest sister had became a devout Christian and returned to her native southern India to teach and make a living. She died suddenly in her late forties, likely the victim of foul play. Aaron made many enquiries through the police to get information on the crime but the police never found who had murdered her or had a role in her murder. This older sister's love of jewellery and gifts of beautiful clothes (traditional style) for her nieces was a family joke to Aaron's side of the family but endeared her to my mother and aunt, her nieces. They kept the pieces of jewellery they received from her taking them into their marriages and later lives. And that love of jewellery was to play a part in my aunt's and my own love of collecting modern and antique jewellery.

Hope's world shrank with the losses of her sisters, the poison of deception practiced by the missionaries and police, followed by deceitful men in Germany, the discrimination and patronage by religious people (such as bishops, pastors and missionaries) and the administrative bureaucrats of British India. The overwhelming grief and sadness were never to leave her. She became a victim to rheumatoid arthritis (an auto-immune disease) in her late thirties which crippled her joints and bones causing her unbearable pain, leaving her weeping and wanting death. She survived as a bed-ridden husk of a woman, crippled with pain which was written large in her eyes, face and body which would last for twenty years. Her social and community work diminished as she prayed to her Christian god asking for release from the life of pain and sadness. Her pain was to infect subsequent generations, including her daughters and son and their children and grandchildren. The stolen child, who had watched Hailey's comet with awe, had internalised the sadness which spread through her body and took hold of every cell of her being. Today, somatic psychotherapy and many other body-aware therapies would recognise this pain as symptomatic of PTSD (post-traumatic stress disorder) and chronic anxiety and depression.

My memories of her are as a woman of compassion and sadness. Her charity now extended to the people who came to her home; never did a beggar or person with a request go away empty-handed or unfulfilled. My grandfather continued to be the kind and philanthropic man that he was and Hope gave him all her support. I remember her as a woman who sat on the front veranda during the day for hours, her eyes fixed far away – in her own inner world. She would tell us stories of distant times and her constant exhortation was 'live a good life and do good to others'. From a feisty, independent, strong-willed woman, who had defied convention in favour of the moral, conscientious choice, she turned into a mild-mannered, misty-eyed saint. Hence my comparison of her spirit to that of Mirabai, the Indian saint who devoted her life to her god and singing his praises.

She died when I was nine. We were living in a place a few hundred miles away from where my grandparents lived . Besides her bones which had turned brittle and chalky, her lungs had given up on her and given rise to pneumonia and other lung diseases. She would sit up as much as she could to ease her lungs and one day fell asleep as she sat on the edge of her bed. Falling onto a tiled floor, she broke both her legs. Put into plaster, she cried about the further pain she was suffering. Her family knew she would not survive long and she died two weeks later at the age of fifty-six. Her death made the headlines in two local newspapers as 'Prominent Social Worker dies'. My mother and her siblings were at the funeral, heartbroken at the death of this good and saintly woman.

Hundreds came to her funeral. Her epitaph could have been encapsulated in the words of a middle-aged man who came to the funeral and wept brokenly. When asked, he told my mother and aunt this story. Thirty years before, he was married to a good woman but they had no children. They discovered that his wife had a dreadful lung disease and needed to be hospitalised but they were very poor and had no material means. My grandmother came to hear of their story and visited their home, asking to meet with them. In despair, this man had not wanted to let his wife go, fearing she would never return. Hope convinced him to let her take his wife to a recognised hospital for treatment. The woman went into a sanatorium to get better and stayed there for almost a year. Hope visited the woman diligently and also talked to the man regularly to keep his hopes alive. Once the woman was released in good health, Hope accompanied her back to her home to a joyful reunion with her husband. The couple went on to have a few children, making their joy complete. My mother, aunt, uncle and grandfather listened to his story teary-eyed and amazed. They had not known the extent of Hope's good works which she had always done in a way as to draw no attention just as suggested in the Sermon on the Mount: 'When you give to the needy, do not let your left hand know what your right hand is doing' (Matthew 6:3, KJV)

Her compassion and kindness along with Aaron's was to have a lasting impact on me. Their example of modesty and unpretentious way of helping people (not wanting to draw attention to themselves) would always resonate with me. Recently, some friends said to me that I can be too humble (I think they meant too modest) at times. But that's the way it should be. Would it not be tantamount to blowing your own trumpet? Why should we draw attention to our grand deeds thus defeating the purpose of service and compassion?

To me, Hope's life embodies the words in a report on Indigenous children who were stolen from their parents and their native community. It seems that children who are removed at critical periods of their lives need someone to take on the role of mother. They don't know how to auto-regulate or soothe themselves nor do they know how to turn off their emotions. Some of these children enter emotional states that are turned off and indifferent to the world around them and unresponsive to those who would comfort them. Many have a haunted, faraway look in their eyes. Just as I saw in my grandmother, because like her they have given up all hope of finding their parents again.

Apparently, children suffering from early trauma also release a stress hormone that kills cells in the hippocampus of the brain. This makes learning and long-term memory difficult and predisposes them to stress-related illnesses for the rest of their lives. It would seem that trauma in infancy can lead to a type of super-sensitisation which can last into adulthood.

Children of parents who lost loved ones often grow up with ghosts, meaning that missing family members are psychologically present but physically absent. While parents may know exactly whom they have lost, their children know very little of their parents and lose their connection to their clan and a lot of their family history.

Reports on stolen children or those taken from their parents without permission and then fostered out show that parents pass their traumas on to their children. As in Australia and its Indigenous stolen generations, trauma is transferred from one generation to the next. Families and children of the stolen children are impacted with the same sense of trauma, grief and loss.

I called my grandmother, Naani, which means maternal grandmother in Hindi. In this account, you will have read that trauma would be visited on her children in one form or another. My mother, her second daughter, was to express this inter-generational trauma not just in the form of sadness but also anger. I saw her express both sorrow and anger on many occasions. According to some psychologists, anger is depression turned inwards whenever she contemplated or underwent any form of loss including thoughts regarding the probable loss of her husband in army manoeuvres or loss of control over her children when they rebelled or played up. Her initial solution, likely unconscious, was to fall in love with my father in the belief that this man from her mother's part of the country would redeem and sustain her with his strength and valour, take her away from her lovely surroundings to something more exotic thus erasing the terrifying pictures of losing her mother and way of life she had enjoyed from her brain. But these unconscious desires for mitigation of loss and release from pain and sadness would lead her to fall in love a second time - with religion fundamentalist beliefs - as a way of ensuring that God would be kind to her in this and the next.

MY WISE AND WONDERFUL GRANDFATHER – TEACHER AND ROLE MODEL

I said I learnt compassion, mercy, kindness, generosity, modesty and humility from him my grandparents, parents and other forbears, which includes my maternal grandparents, my parents, my aunts and various nannies and family friends who had a role in my upbringing. They were gracious people – that aptly descriptive word is now forgotten and not much used except when describing the Queen or some illustrious member of the old nobility – though not the ones who figured in recent accounts of those who threw disgraceful tantrums.

I called my grandfather *Naana,* which is the Hindi or Urdu term for maternal grandfather. When I think of my grandfather, whom I shall call Aaron, I visualise him as the noblest, most compassionate and forward-thinking man of his time. The meaning of life and the most valued human qualities mattered deeply to him from his youth onwards . For him and his wife (whom I have called Hope) who shared his sentiments, 'doing good' was a religion in itself. Many a time he told me that 'service to others' had been his motto from his teenage years onwards. Though considered well-to-do by Indian standards (upper-middle-class), their manners and way of being embodied helping and serving the community and giving freely of their wits, time, contacts, money and whatever influence they possessed. This is not to say that I did not see him angry from time to time but his anger was to do with being disappointed or let down in his values or expectations of us and others. His anger was not about small things – not having a clean shirt or not having enough rupees in his wallet. This anger, which I seem to have inherited, was about being short-changed; about not being told the truth; about people lying or hood-winking him; about people's lack of good manners. I learnt more about morals and social graces, about generosity and giving graciously from my grandparents than anyone else.

My grandfather was a Christian man, who was committed to community service both as an official of the YMCA in northern India and also through his role as Welfare & Personnel Manager of the group of industrial mills in that city. He had other roles in the community and he took all these roles and duties very seriously. He employed kindness, justice and morality in a very balanced way and many a person came to his door seeking his help in matters of justice and fairness and cutting through the tapes of bureaucracy. He also happened to be the ersatz family head of his eight siblings and their now aged parents. Aaron's father, David, had been a doctor, following in the footsteps of his adoptive missionary father. David had been discovered as a seven-year old along with his five-year old brother, wandering around in a village where everyone had died due to dysentery and cholera. They were adopted by the medical missionary and his wife who rescued them and both boys took on their missionary father's surname. Aaron's mother had been a young Sikh woman, the only daughter in a family with many sons, who went to an English school in northern India and then, under missionary persuasion, chose to become a Christian. Her name was changed to Naomi and she married my great-grandfather, David, and went on to have eight children, composed of six boys and two girls.

Aaron was born in 1898 in a remote part of Afghanistan which was then part of an undivided India. He was the second child of his parents. His father had become a doctor, following in the footsteps of his adoptive medical missionary parents, and served in this remote part of the country. He was clever, open-minded and resourceful; he also loved listening to stories of yesteryear from people living around him. He had a store of such stories and traditional lore and would tell us wonderful stories with great gusto. I think I owe my own memories and knowledge of our heritage and of India in the late 19th and early 20th centuries to my grandfather. He did very well at school and seemed to have been the go-getter in the family. After finishing school, he went on to college, obtaining a Bachelor's degree in humanities at a university in Punjab province of undivided northern India under British rule. Towards the end of Wold War I, at age 19, he volunteered for service. While not a conscientious objector, he preferred to serve people and applied for and got a role as a Chaplain for troops serving in the middle-east, Mesopotamia, as he told me.

He was also a lover of history and archaeology and hence it was a privilege for him to serve in the lands where so much history had happened over millennia and where the great war was raging. He returned to his native India, at the end of the war, deeply touched by the bloodshed and suffering and determined to serve his fellow human beings. He joined the YMCA and remained a lifelong member. Soon he was looking for and getting jobs which entailed being sent to various parts of India to serve in a Welfare Officer capacity. This, I think, meant he worked in communities or with organisations, either employer- owned or Government-sponsored services, where people toiled and needed education, employment and better communal facilities.

He married Hope in 1921, and went to live in a town in central India, for a few years doing the work that he loved. Soon, he had a daughter, my aunt, followed by another girl, my mother. Strangely, he was turning away from Anglo-Saxon names and changed his own surname to an Indian one. He started giving his children Hindu and Sanskrit names as they rightfully lived in a land filled with history and one of the most ancient religions in the world - Hinduism. He understood that giving children Anglo names could denote that the person belonged to a subordinate culture; such Anglo names may indicate that he was a 'rice' Christian as many Indians before and after him had given up their names, religions and histories to get some food on the plate; also the day of freedom, equalisation and independence was not too far away. He did go to a Protestant church and respected everything Christian and human but his heart was committed to serving his fellow humans. He often quoted a bible verse to me 'how can you say you love god whom you have never seen when you cannot love your brother whom you have seen.' (1 John 4:20, KJV)

He immersed himself in philanthropy, serving on the boards of several community service organisations. He was also appointed an Honorary Magistrate, an Honorary Jail Visitor, and was a leading member of various city safety committees and land grant committees for low income earners, the YMCA, literacy and hygiene committees, and a mover of and then a patron of a large housing settlement (a community housing board) for low-income workers.

His work was recognised by the British rulers of India by giving him various offices and at times sending him to places where community work was needed. It seems to have been a top-down approach but Aaron incorporated teaching people both their letters as well as transferable work skills into their activities. By the late 1920s, he had another child, a son, and the family moved to a city in northern India where they would live for the next forty years and he would become a pillar of the community.

His deep interest in religion particularly Hinduism and Indian culture led him to research and write a book about Hindu beliefs and rituals which was published in the 1930s and was available till a few years ago. I understand it was still in print eighty years later though it has re-printed and published under a different soft-cover.

As part of the British masters' recognition, Aaron was invited to go to Europe in the mid-1930s to visit and learn of ways that people were working. He went to London, Paris, Geneva and later to various places in Germany to listen and learn. This was a three month trip; Aaron and Hope went by rail to Mumbai, then by ocean liner to London via the Suez Canal. They saw many strange and interesting sights and were treated graciously by most of their peers and fellow travellers. He met with many of the luminaries in the YMCA in Britain. They travelled by boat to France, then train to Paris and later Geneva, returning by way of Germany, visiting places recommended by people in the YMCA movement and the British-German Friendship League who were also part of many of the community service activities in which Aaron was interested. This led to visits of workers camps (which is how the concentration camps were then named), as well as new ideas in hygiene, sanitation and feeding people. The Europeans and British friends and well-wishers were very kind and hospitable to them and they returned three months later to northern India, mostly satisfied that they had been to see the English and European world, that they both admired and loved.

Hope however was not very happy (having left her children, my mother and her siblings, to be looked after by the Principal of the school where they studied) and her latent sadness, anxiety and an attack of food poisoning on board the ship led to her being confined to bed with what turned out to be rheumatoid arthritis (an auto-immune disease). Hope's story which appears earlier in this book includes a more detailed account of their visit to Germany, including a visit to a work camp (later discovered to be the site of an internment or concentration camp). The news of *Kristallnacht*, the onset of World War II and subsequent discoveries in Germany as the war ended was to tear the blinkers from Aaron's eyes and make him realise that he had been duped by their German friends and well-wishers.

Grandpa Aaron spent the rest of the war period working in community projects and in welcoming, hosting and 'entertaining' service men in addition to his other community activities. On one occasion, Aaron took his daughters, my mother and aunt, to a movie-entertainment function which is how my mother and father met. My mother wanted to marry him immediately but Aaron put in a condition – only if you finish your under-graduate studies. This said, my mother who was always a Grade 1 student, slipped into the 'B' category and managed to get a 2nd class undergraduate degree while she spent many hours a day 'dreaming' about the man she wanted to marry. Dad was a Flying Officer in the Royal Indian Air Force, having received his commission as an officer by the British rulers of India, as part of their affirmative action plan. My parents' love affair consisted of short letters and telegrams written by Dad and long letters written by my mother till they could marry in May 1945 as the war drew to a close. The biggest obstacle was to be their religions (she a Christian, he a high-class Hindu), which they would overcome with the help of Grandpa Aaron. They also had different native languages (she spoke Urdu and Hindustani and he spoke Tamil) but they both spoke good English which was to be the basis of their love affair. We grew up speaking two north Indian languages and English from birth.

Despite all of Aaron's broad acceptance of religions and his ecumenical philosophy, which was so unusual for his time, the partition of India would unfold a story of grief and horror to be added to his burden of community and familial service. Dad's active service straight after the war continued as he moved into the army and this meant that he was away on civil policing duties as India grappled with the horror of princely states being acquired and added to the gestating Indian republic. My mother would come 'home' to her parents to have her children, first her older daughter and then later myself while Dad continued his military career as an army officer – engaging in various military actions as rulers of princely states either came over willingly to be a part of the new India or dug their heels in and needed to be 'coaxed' 'won' or bulldozed over to the Indian side. I was born nine days before the actual partition of India – dividing the nation into India and Pakistan. Father was away and my pregnant mother with her oldest child were living with our grandparents.

As India began to be partitioned into two countries, Pakistan and India, Aaron was deeply troubled. He had six brothers and sisters and their families scattered over northern India including the estranged wife (Helen) of one of his brothers, who was living in an area to become part of West Pakistan. His brother was not interested in finding the mother of his three sons but Aaron who took safety in general and the security of family members very seriously told me that he went in search of some of his relatives as India staggered in the bloodbath when the countries divided. Trainloads, busloads and long lines of people marched to borders eastward or westward, seeking protection and security. He felt no fear in himself as he believed he was neutral with his avowed Christianity. He also decided to check on two of his brothers and their families who lived in the Punjab - the state that was being divided between Pakistan and India. And he hoped to ensure the safety of one of his friends who lived in a city in the same province. He got on a train in Delhi going towards the border. The train was crowded beyond belief with people crushed into compartments and sitting on top of railway carriages, full of fear and trepidation at the fate that awaited them. He got off in a town a couple of hundred miles from the new border where some of his brothers and parents lived and was able to find out that the ones he sought were safe and in good health in the little village outside the town. He went back to the station a few hours later and took the next train to the border. Trains were being shunted every which way as troop trains and passenger trains raced in all directions. He got on to a troop train by pulling favours with the Station master and as his train approached the border caught up with the train he had been on the day before. He descended on to the platform in the city prior to the border and a scene of carnage met his eyes. People belonging to one religion lay around on the platform dying or dead, sliced open by the swords of men from the opposing religion who were roaming the station platforms. This beautiful, loving man from whom I was to learn my values of justice, humility, mercy and compassion picked his way through the horror on the platform, through 'rivers of blood' and clumps of flesh as if the vultures and hyenas had feasted and fled. He came across a man he knew, a pastor of a small Christian church, who had converted to Christianity in his very young days. The man lay dying, thirsting for a sip of water, to ease his journey into the next world. He had been put to the sword because he was circumcised, a practice of some religions. Aaron opened his thermos and started to pour a cup of water for him when he was pushed by a man with flashing red eyes and brandishing a blood-streaked sword. 'If you give him a drop of water, you will be the next to feel this blade' said the man. Grandpa hesitated; he knew the man was dying and his merciful cup of water would not save the man. But the fact that he could not help him caused him to feel deep shame. He stopped but berated himself for his lack of moral courage in not defying the man with the sword. He stumbled away from the platform with tears in his eyes, grieving for himself and his dying friend and the vast sins of humanity that he had just witnessed.

As the Partition of India raged, with trains, buses and mile-long crowds of people trampling towards eastern and western borders of India, most families in an area which was predominantly occupied by people of the 'other religion' were on tenterhooks. This was particularly true in areas close to the new borders of India namely West Pakistan and East Pakistan (now Bangladesh). However, families in affluent neighbourhoods felt the pressure less but remained vigilant. Mob rule was in force in the poorer and less educated neighbourhoods, fed by stories of mass atrocities – both real and made-up.

Grandpa Aaron's onward journey was to take him to a city which would become part of Pakistan. He stopped and made enquiries about his sister-in-law, Helen, his brother's estranged wife. She had left his brother a couple of years before, taking two of her younger sons who were 6 and 8 years old, to live with a judge (a man of Hindu extraction) and his family of four daughters. Helen and the judge lived in a small suburb of a town or township, in the sort of idyllic neighbourhood which had preceded the partition of India, where neighbours were bound more by affluence and manners than religion. The people of the neighbourhood were gracious and well-mannered to one another, shared food and dishes at prominent religious festivals of their own and other religions but never went to the point of getting married to one another. On the surface, a well-mannered society where tolerance and respect held sway.

Helen and the Judge lived in such a neighbourhood. Was their relationship more intimate than that of employer and housekeeper-cum- governess to his daughters we will never know. They lived in a small mansion (which had enough bedrooms for the family), household attendants to help with the cooking and housework, a large flower and vegetable garden, a courtyard to meet in and a well for watering the garden. She was reasonably happy, or perhaps she was happy enough as she was still getting over losing all her children in the past few months. Her oldest son, ten years old and living in a far away city in India with his father, had sneaked into the judge's home and kidnapped his two younger brothers when their mother was having an afternoon nap. He had left his home city with no money, riding trains across India (over a course of 3 or 4 days), to snatch his brothers from their mother and return with them to his father in the same far away city. Yes, it was still a patriarchal world and any woman who left a man could expect to have such punishment meted out to her. She could go to court and get a divorce and perhaps an injunction to keep her children but no so-called self-respecting man would abide by a court's decision and let his sons live with their mother. This story of loss and theft of children would resonate in my family for decades.

The judge was away for a couple of days on his circuit to hear cases in rural areas. He also wanted to check on land which he owned in an outlying village, hoping that he could sell it to a neighbouring farmer. This would then make their life easier and if things did not work out, he would have ready cash for them to make the dash to India and live near relatives who had already made the journey. Helen and his daughters were safe in a mansion protected by high walls and a household attendants armed with stout staves. Yet, they lived in an area of the Punjab which had now been ceded to Pakistan (the new nation). The judge instructed Helen to be extra careful and not let anyone they did not know into the house. He would be back with cash or jewels to allow them to go to India if they so decided.

Late afternoon when Helen and the girls were having their siesta, their faithful household *major domo* came to hammer on their bedroom doors. He cried: "Wake up, madam, wake and come quickly. A mob is coming our way. Quick, hide". So they put up a ladder and climbed to the top of the house, which had a crenellated roof about three feet high. The women drew up the ladder and lay on the rooftop, hiding from view. The faithful *major domo* guarded the front door as the mob approached. He had been instructed to give them money and valuables so as to divert them, telling them that he was in charge as the judge and his family were away. He went to the door but was not successful in deterring the mob. They smashed their way into the house, took the money and jewellery, broke the furniture, looted the kitchen pantry and cupboards but they wanted the women. One in the mob cried: 'We know the judge is away because he took his car and chauffeur out of town yesterday but his women were not with him. Where are they? Tell us, or we will kill you too. The old *major domo* stood initially at the front door and then near the back door trying to reason with the crowd but his efforts were met with more hostility and brandishing of sharp knives and stout sticks. Helen and the girls who were hiding on the open roof-top could hear what was going on and trembled for their lives. Finally, they decided to lower the ladder into the inner courtyard of the house, near the old jasmine vine and descended as quietly as possible. They would not be seen from the main garden. As they descended, there was a roar from the mob as they hacked the poor *major domo* to death for denying them access to the women. He was a man of a different faith but one who revered his master, the Judge and his women-folk which also included Helen. In the uproar, the women unanimously made up their minds to stop the mob from raping and killing them, choosing to jump into the old well at the very back of the courtyard which was used for watering the gardens. The five women, rather one woman and four young girls (teenagers and younger) threw themselves into the well just as the courtyard doors were broken open and the mob poured into the inner courtyard. They killed themselves to preserve their 'virtue' and to avoid the long and terrifying rape and torture that would follow.

A day later, Aaron arrived in the village to meet the judge who had just returned from his circuit work. He had managed to sell his small-holding in a faraway village for a very small amount only to come home and find it looted and his housekeeper-life partner and daughters dead. The Judge was never to be the same again. He agreed to accompany my grandfather eastward from divided Punjab to India but would die soon after a sick and broken man.

This would shock Aaron to the core - the evil that men could do to each other. He would return to the home-town on the Ganges River where I would be born a few days later, deeply shaken and sad beyond belief. In the week before I was born, he said he had fulfilled another of his duties as a Jail Visitor to see a man who was accused of murder. The hanging of the man was due in the next week, very likely on the day of my birth, but his eyes, according to Grandpa Aaron, were already empty, vacant, dead. His heart and spirit were broken and hanging was only a formality. Aaron resigned from this community service position as he could neither take the lack of mercy nor the extremity of the punishment.

Another shock awaited him in the coming months. Months after World War II ended, Aaron and Hope were sitting on the front veranda when they saw a gaunt, emaciated man with a long beard walk up the driveway. His walk was familiar but his face was not. As he came closer, Aaron jumped up and ran to embrace him. It was one of his brothers, who had volunteered to serve in the Armed Forces. He had been sent to the east, was captured by the Japanese and ended in prison in Far East. Later, along with many other British and allied troops, he was sent to work on building an infamous railway. During the war, no news was ever received of him nor any mention of his welfare. Aaron and the rest of the family thought he had been killed and buried in an unmarked grave. He had survived the war but prison and the forced labour on the building of the railway had left an indelible mark on him. He was ravaged by the horrific bouts of dysentery, cholera and other wasting diseases that he had gone through. He was in shock when he was released but made his way home to his brother and family, where he recuperated for a very long time. His health was never the same again but he could neither talk of the war nor of his suffering.

Aaron was thankful that his future son-in-law had survived World War II. My father had seen service in the eastern parts of India and the Far East, as Britain prepared to defend this area from the Japanese advancement. I think Aaron's thankfulness at seeing my father safe at the end of the War led him to agree to let my parents get married. I don't think he could have got over his daughter's heartbreak if my father had been wounded or killed. (My father was a young Hindu officer in the Air Force and Aaron's daughter, my mother, was a young, educated and well brought-up Christian woman. Their stories appear earlier in this book.)

Though Aaron had a college education, I remember he continued his education on a lifelong basis. This trait of his affected my mother and aunt as well as my siblings and myself. He read copiously and I can remember his study being lined with bookshelves with lots of books of all sorts, ranging from history to philosophy, archaeology to religious tomes, Ripley's Believe it or not, classics as well as general knowledge books. He also stayed in touch with the world at large – three daily newspapers were delivered to his home along with at least six or seven magazines a week – from the Illustrated Weekly of India, the Spectator, News of the World (however late they came to India), Reader's Digest, National Geographic just to mention a few. He set me on my path of reading books as they came across my lap, buying me books for birthdays including those which may not be considered very appropriate for children including 'Arabian Nights' (rather hot and sexy), world stories in outline and full editions,

Encyclopaedias including one of Greek gods and goddesses and their Roman counterparts (which stole my imagination). I got to read 'Jane Eyre', 'Wuthering Heights', 'Tess of the d'Urbervilles', 'The Brothers Karamazov', 'Pride and Prejudice', 'Utopia' along with ghost stories and some age appropriate comics (though he did not approve of the latter). Some of my happiest memories consist of sitting in the garage in a stationary car at the height of summer (110 degrees Fahrenheit or 43 degrees Celsius!) reading past copies of Readers' Digests, National Geographic and many of the older books and magazines which lined the built-in shelves of the garage.

His travels during World War I and then later in Europe had woken in him a love of travel. He would make his arrangements quietly and without fuss and one day he would say, I am off to Kolkata or Mumbai this week. Surprised, we would ask: "Why, Grandpa, where are you going?" "Oh, I think I will visit my sisters and brothers and then I will take a plane to Hong Kong or a ship to Japan". And we, like the rest of the family and his friends would be somewhat stunned. Another time, he said he was off to Germany to relive some of his old memories but in a country which was now recovering from and making reparations for the bad that had happened. He took many trips to Europe and to the East; of course, he travelled all over India from the snowy mountains in the north to the extreme south. He had a restless, yearning spirit and taking in the new and understanding how the world was changing was his way of coming to terms with the pace of his life and that of his country.

Besides travel, he took care to learn languages. One of his trips consisted of joining a group which would study and speak Esperanto to one another all through the journey. He had learnt French, German and Spanish. He spoke at least five north-western Afghani languages plus Urdu and English. I remember he spoke ten languages with some facility and ease. He asked me to study and learn the Arabic script in which Urdu is written. Over the course of one hot summer, he taught me the Arabic alphabet and then set about making me read primary and secondary style of books. Then it was on to reading the Bible in Urdu and until I could read the Psalms fluently I was not let off the hook. He begged me to keep up my language skills but I have forgotten much of the Arabic script and now look around vainly for someone to teach me to read the Arabic script so that I can honour the memory of this wonderful man.

He had many pro bono community responsibilities such as being the representative for international care organisations in northern India; giving time and effort into employment and re-skilling of impoverished communities where he lived. His daughters and their families went away to other states to live and he was only able to visit them occasionally. As he grew older he needed more care and a bit of coddling. He had been a widower for over ten years and decided to get a housekeeper with a young daughter to look after him and his big house. This caused a big flap with his two daughters and his grandson - my brother- who had come to live with him while he attended college in the town. Whether there was a liaison or not, I don't know but I do know that he was lonely and often wrote of missing our voices and pranks from the time we had lived with him. I think my mother and aunt (true to their late mother's memory) prevailed on him to get rid of the housekeeper and her daughter. I think he did but later then decided to pack up and leave the town where he had spent over forty years of his life and go to live in a place in another state where his own parents had lived for a while. He built a small house on a piece of land and lived in a much reduced state. His health started to deteriorate and he did not last five years in this new life in the village.

On a trip to visit his older daughter in the city where she lived, his health problems caused him to land in hospital with kidney and heart problems which led to other major health issues. At this time, my parents decided that Grandpa would come to live with them. He was sliding into dementia and would not last long, dying at the age of seventy-seven.

In a nutshell, I think of him as the hero and role model in my life. He was gracious and held the highest values that he knew among which were giving to those who did not have, caring for others, taking up the voices and concerns of those who could not voice their own causes. I learned from him the values of being modest and compassionate, never upstaging others, never putting people down and always putting others first. He was enormously knowledgeable and well-connected but never belittled those who did not have the same skills and resources.

I know love and longing and the miraculous veil time creates can blind us to people's shortcomings. He had his faults – he was strict in all maters to do with cleanliness and hygiene; at times he became irascible when we (children) irritated him with our clowning and racketing around the house. He was also a student of human behaviour and shared his beliefs with his family and friends (if they were willing to listen) on morality, social mores and how to be a force for good in the world. For a man who rose from humble beginnings he never lost his modesty but remained compassionate and helpful to all he met.

I learnt from him layers of social mores regarding hospitality, giving graciously, being a caring host, using his networks and contacts to help people who needed help and support to get ahead, table-manners and how to behave in polite society. His courage and outspokenness combined with his modesty stay in my mind and heart as living examples. More than these virtues I think he was imbued by the zeitgeist of his times – he was a patriot and community worker at many levels - deeply affected by the work of people who are considered the patriots and fathers of modern India including Mahatma Gandhi, Jawaharlal Nehru, Vallabhai Patel and many others.

His wisdom, compassionate leadership and truly liberated views on women, the people less educated and ones who did not have the means of life have guided my life. Like Dad, he was an accidental and unknowing 'feminist' – he fought tirelessly for his daughters and their female friends to have a college education. He supported them in their beliefs and philosophies like a wise father and a gracious mentor. This was unheard of in India and perhaps in most other countries in the nineteen thirties and forties but his values and beliefs would not allow him to favour his son with the material goods of life and a first-class education if his daughters did not get the same. His daughters and grand-daughters were given the freedom to have equal voices and to follow their independent ways. He would remain a just and gracious man all his life.

I feel sad that I did not have more interaction and communication with him in the later years of his life. I was trying to make my way as a wife and later as a mother and though I wrote to him fairly regularly, I wish I had visited him more, and understood his loneliness and lack of company. Alas, those were the days before social media and the ubiquitous telephone took over our lives.

LETTER TO MY DAUGHTER

I had not expected to fall in love with anyone so devotedly and whole-heartedly. In my teens, I was convinced about the futility and tiresomeness of true love. I did not read romance novels and did not believe in it. However, you had not come into my life and I was not to know that love would enter my heart insidiously and trap me in the strongest web possible. So, you should know that before you were born, I was lonely and often desperate. I had entered a marriage which I felt I was supposed to enter because it was right, convenient and ticked all the right boxes; however, it was in a marriage that had not fulfilled any of my social, spiritual or emotional dreams but that is a separate story.

In my teens and early twenties, I often looked into my psyche but did not think of myself as a maternal or longing for motherhood. At other times, I tried to imagine being a mother but could not waken the deep feelings that other women are said to have. I thought I was not meant to be a mother or bring up another generation. I was lost in terms of a familial role – I had been a daughter and wife but neither understood nor been in the role of another sort.

Then I became pregnant as if by accident. When you were born and you were put into my arms, I looked at you and thought you were the most beautiful yet fragile person I had ever seen. A spark of love began to grow in me and soon it was a small flame. I can still feel it - fragrant and warm like the skin on your neck - smelling of gardenias and milk - when I kissed you. Your thick, dark hair stood up on end when I first saw you but soon it began to flatten out and months later it became wavy. You were and still are so beautiful. And your eyes were the most startlingly beautiful part of you. Large, dark, brown and full of knowledge and wisdom. They peered into my heart and made indelible marks on my soul.

You were perfect in every way. The doctor who delivered you said that you would be timid when he saw you a month after your birth. But you were vulnerable, just making your way in the world. Once you were confident, you began to grow into your larger than life personality - of truth, justice, being outspoken and individualistic – your very own way of life. Today, you are an intelligent confident, articulate and outspoken woman who makes her views and beliefs known without fear or favour.

Did you know that I had to argue and dodge my way around in giving you your name? Your father wanted to name you after previous girl-friends which I refused to agree to. Nor was I allowed to give you an Indian name. Finally, I agreed to a simple first and second name. They are good solid names and reflect the justice and satisfaction you bring to me and those of who love and trust you.

In your own special way, caring for you made my 'femaleness' come to life again. As a mother, I would gaze at you a lot (and no, you couldn't put obstacles such as bottles of water between us to stop me looking at you) as you gurgled and burbled and drank and ate and played and slept. Your aches and pains and groans became mine. The rash on your neck when you had to be clothed in a woollen vest in the middle of summer became my cross! I became a sneak for you, tearing it off as soon as the coast was clear and putting it on the last minute (while the fan forced cool air over you) when our persecutor arrived. Thanks to an alert doctor, who laid down the law, we could put that damn woollen vest away and you never had to wear it again.

Your forthright, outspoken nature – lover of truth and justice and lifter-upper of the downtrodden – showed itself early. We had been to the consulate for an interview and it was apparent that the consular official did not favour people of colour entering the country. While your father fawned and smiled and banked on his colour and race to get him over the hurdles, you sat there at one month of age gazing unblinkingly at him. When the official started to patronise me and ask whether I would be able to fit into the western way of life, your gut began to rumble. You still gazed at him unflinchingly while I went into parallel meltdown with you revolted wondering about the uncivilised people I had stumbled into. Then you broke wind, unleashing a cyclone of sulphur dioxide, several times, teaching the patronising fool not to mess with you and me.

As a baby you seemed to prefer males to females. When we stayed with my parents for three months you developed a deep affection for your grandfather and would chase him on your hands and knees to be picked up and carried around the veranda and garden. You chose him to care for you when I developed an eye infection and could not care for you for many days.

Journeying to Australia opened up new possibilities for you. You were only nine months old but loved the strangeness of airports and new places, swivelling around to look at every new thing like a 'twirly' toy. You took Bangkok, Hong Kong, Darwin, Sydney in your stride and soon began your explorations. Television was new and so was the play school program. Soon you had me galloping through our little apartment on a broomstick (perhaps I was the witch chasing you on your steed); excavating drawers and pulling things out to find new adventures and once in a big department store to un-harnessing yourself from your stroller and disappearing up an escalator! My racing heart and screams of terror showed me what it would mean to lose you. I felt my heart had been ripped out and torn to shreds. Your appeared fifteen minutes later with a security guard having been found examining crayons and pencils in another department. Were you thinking of writing your novella or opera even then?

You showed your kindness and compassion early which made me love you even more. I was so depressed – not just due to homesickness but yearning for people who loved me and finding it difficult to make my way in a strange land. Tormented by a man who wanted to get rid of me and take you away to another country, I would sit and cry for hours in a corner of your playroom and sometimes bang my head on the wall. You would come over and pat me on the shoulder or kiss me on the cheek to comfort me. How did you know what to do when you were only eighteen months old? You became my shining light in the middle of a dark world.

Yet you loved your father so much. He played with you and gave you a lot of love. That became my secret burden and remains a source of huge inner conflict. You were not mine alone I knew then and even now. But the fork in the road was choosing between being put into a psychiatric ward and losing you entirely or raising myself from my sick bed despite my depression, loneliness and glandular fever and finding a place for us to hide. Your very being and the love you gave me would keep me alive and help me to save you from being tormented and changed into a tormented young woman as you grew up. That's what I believed then and still do.

I left once. And I was dragged back. I left again and went to USA with you but duty brought me back to Australia. Soon after you were forcibly taken away by your father and I knew I had to do things properly. I determined to get custody of you so that I could bring you up legally and lovingly in a way you richly deserved. It took me two years after that till I got myself an administrative job and began to look for accommodation, which I finally found with a feisty German woman with a heart of gold, who also offered to look after you before and after school, all for a tiny sum. My heart glowed with love and thankfulness because 'freedom' was in sight. Finally I had a reason for living: in fact, I made a vow to myself at that time to stay alive till you became eighteen so that I could always protect and look after you.

We came to live at our new friend's place, someone we met through a local church. I got custody of you so long as I never left the Sydney metropolitan area. We started to build a life. You went to the local primary school and played with our housemate's children after school. However, every second weekend you would go to see your father and often you came home with tears in your eyes, often crying for your own pain and sometimes screaming abuse at me. I knew what was happening. Your heart was being broken by having to listen to arguments and abuse about the other parent, something which no one should have to listen to and no parent should ever do to a child. Every child needs the space to develop their own love and loyalty and the freedom to grow up in a caring, loving and non-argumentative household, where there is no tug-of-war for exclusive loyalty. This went on for a few years – sometimes, you went for months without seeing your father and at other times it was regular, alternate weekends. It broke my heart to watch as someone almost broke your spirit. I am sorry I could not help you more. I grieve for the pain it caused you.

You grew up and showed your intelligence and creativity at school. You were tested and 'labelled' a Gifted Child. Your reading and mathematical age was three to four years beyond your biological age. You became talented at drama and developed musical skills.

I am sorry I disappointed you at times; I did not come to serve in the school canteen or attend the Easter Hat Parade or give stuff to the children's charity; I actually did not understand the meaning and significance of those occasions and due to being a 9-to-5 worker could not come and serve in the canteen and become friends with other mothers and allow you to swell with pride because you had a mother, who served in the canteen. However, many of your teachers in primary school spoke of you fondly and admiringly. Many said it was a joy to have you in their class; your brightness and willingness to engage and learn was a boon to many a teacher who struggled to get a class to learn and develop. You were the great sponge who sucked it all in, added your own intelligence and insight and leapfrogged to a higher frame. I was and still am so proud of you. I am in awe of your insight, intelligence and breathtaking creativity among so many other accomplishments and qualities.

Time passed; you went to a local High School in Sydney and began to grow into a sparkling and beautiful teenager. You were blossoming and I looked forward to my evenings and weekends with you. I was sad when I had to have someone look after you in school holidays when our dear friend and housemate was not available. And then I re-married (for my own reasons) which you did not like but went along with me for peace and harmony. I had to coax you to come to live in Melbourne and start another life making new friends. Soon you did and also became very 'religious', studying the Bible and getting baptised. I was determined to let you make your own decisions. I came to some of the services in the church because I wanted to support you and I am glad I did so.

In Melbourne, you were initially sad because of the bullying at your first school. You even played 'hooky' staying home from school because of the bad treatment you had received. I am glad I found out and somehow we managed to get you back on track. Which led you to the school of your dreams and there you found your passion in life. Music and being creatively involved in composition and playing music. You found a new best friend in a girl with the same name as yourself and started friendships with young men. You had another life of which I was vaguely aware but I was glad you were finding your own interests and blossoming. And then I had to find another job, which led us both back to Sydney. You hated that fact and decided to stay in Melbourne for a few more months before coming back to live in our new home in Sydney. The local high school was not your cup of tea; you decided to drop music as an act of rebellion which made me sad and you took a while to make new friends. You were sad at times which made me sad too. You got through your Higher School Certificate at the end of High School but decided not to go on to college. It took a lot of persuasion on my part to get you to go to college (university). Despite taking the HSC casually, you obtained entry marks to get into undergraduate Economics & Law, but you decided to major in Social Studies due to your burning desire to create social justice. Whatever, it took to make you happy was good by me too.

We had a grand twenty-first birthday party for you. Food, drink and lots of friends from school and college and the local church. You were into your element opening bottles of champagne using the French method, which meant with the blunt edge of a knife. Then, the week after your birthday, when you told me you were leaving the family home, I felt sad in losing you. I understood what the 'empty nest syndrome' meant. You started working in a field which was fuelled by your strongly held views of social justice and an active conscience. You worked with people with disabilities first in support and community work, then in inspection, project management and funding, and advising on key areas to rectify current issues. I learned from you at every step of the way. I am sure you did not know this but many a time I quoted you to colleagues and friends, using your reasoning and philosophy in areas ranging from disability rights to women's needs and current injustices affecting minority groups that cried out to be corrected.

During this time, you collaborated with a photographer and mounted an exhibition on the lives and loves of people with disability – photographically and through art installations. Then came a stint with Community Services and I believe you gave it both your heartfelt and critical judgement and support. You also worked with non-government organisations in Disability support and I know you spoke up on many occasions for the rights and protections of those who could not protect or speak for themselves. At times, you did not care to protect yourself from those who did not feel as deeply as you did for the rights of people who lived with disadvantage.

You have gone on to work in tourism, public relations and marketing to bring some great natural wonders in Australia to people's attention. Most of your work has been with not-for-profit organisations providing them with innovative, respectful and people-friendly material and strategies to showcase their organisations. You have been respected for your talent and skills though lesser-talented people may not have taken kindly to you. For years, you have worked diligently in writing programs as well as stories and narratives of Indigenous Australians for which you received scant acknowledgement. That seems to be both your talent and trap – to put in your shining best which leaves many overwhelmed but afraid to acknowledge it. Isn't Australia known for its way of cutting down tall poppies?

You continue to work in music, drama and theatre. Your great opus in the lives and stories of multi-cultural Australia is under construction. You have written multi-hued and emotion-laden lyrics of the lives of women and men who have not had a voice – people from around the world and also Indigenous Australians. You have told me that one of the stories in your musical opus is based on my life. Thank you, my dear daughter, thank you. Your social values and conscience are strong and you combine them with your vast intelligence and musical and lyrical talents to this endeavour. I hope and pray it is a musical which will inspire change in the way people not only treat each other – bringing compassion and respect – but also value the talents, knowledge and wisdom brought by people of many diasporas to Australia.

I don't want to say too much more about you because I respect your privacy. Let me just say that I have got more from you than I have given to you. I have learned about love, care and respect from you; in the bargain, I have also got a wide education from being with you and listening to you on topics as wide apart as disability rights to social media to post-modernism. You have opened my eyes and ears to so many things – particularly human injustices and how live and act in this brave new world.

You have continued to inspire me. Every time I talk to you, I gain another nugget of wisdom to add to my knowledge. Then I do more research into the topic we have talked of and I am amazed at the number of times you have not only been correct but pointed me in new directions and a new understanding . Sometimes when we have argued, you have been cross with me but under all that verbiage I detect genuine love and respect. You may not think so but I always go away uplifted and 'educated' after our dialogues on various current topics.

I see changes and patterns in you over the years. You have gone from being a firebrand with a huge intelligence and a vast array of talents - ranging from music to project management to marketing to consulting on difficult issues - to a mature woman who combines her intelligence with deep inner kindness along with a knowledge of others, insights into human behaviours and self-awareness.

I hope you will follow your starry dreams to full reality. The world is changing just as it did when your great-grandmother saw Halley's Comet in the night skies of southern India. It led her to a different reality but she kept the core of her social values and the care and compassion for others. In my own way, I have had my dreams fulfilled under the southern skies as I have followed my star to its natural zenith. I am positive when Halley's Comet or any other comet or shooting star comes again you will have fulfilled all you envisioned for yourself.

QUESTIONS AND REFLECTIONS ARISING FROM THIS BOOK

1. Did the subjects and experiences of racism, sexism and ageism challenge or unsettle you?
2. Does viewing behaviours through the lens of racism change your view of racial dynamics?
3. Does the concept of sexism or misogyny or the ways that violence towards women is practiced resonate with you? Have you got similar experiences?
4. How can your discomfort help you to examine assumptions and stereotypes that you may have made or those made about you?
5. Have experiences of violence, harassment, racism, sexism and any sort of abuse made you feel shame or embarrassment or less than human?
6. Was the subject of fundamentalist religious behaviours by males towards females (as described in the book) confronting?
7. Have you had experiences of family violence that have shamed and hurt you? How can you find your voice and tell your story?
8. How can you do so, safely - without traumatising yourself? Are their counsellors or groups or organisations which can help you on this journey?

9. Do you believe assertiveness and self-esteem work can be useful to us in finding a place of peace?
10. Did you find the description of intersectional feminism useful and comparable to your own understanding and experiences?

REFERENCES

1. Brian Fung, The Washington Post, January 2018
2. Jesse Oliver, Poet and winner of the Australian Slam Poetry Award 2017, On becoming himself. https://www.gettyimages.com.au/collaboration/boards/sw5nT6pDLEek3iOeSdYMZw
3. Moustafa Bayoumi "How Does It Feel to Be a Problem? Being Young and Arab in America" 2008.
4. IWDA definition of intersectional feminism 2018 https://iwda.org.au/what-does-intersectional-feminism-actually-mean/)
5. Reni Eddo-Lodge Why I'm No Longer Talking to White People about Race', 30 May 2017
6. Dr Peggy MacIntosh 'White Privilege: Unpacking the Invisible Knapsack' (1989)
7. Robin DiAngelo, 'White Fragility – Why it's so hard for white people to talk about racism' 2018
8. Shakti Butler *Mirrors of Privilege: Making Whiteness Visible film*
9. Phoolan Devi, 'I, Phoolan Devi: Autobiography of India's Bandit Queen', 1996
10. Dr. Kevin Leman 'The Birth Order Book' (1998).
11. Brad Parks, *Say Nothing*,2017
12. Dr. Lenore Walker, The 'Cycle of Violence' 1979
13. Carl Rogers, Dr. '*Client Centred Therapy*' 1951
14. Lisa Marchiano, quoted in the DailyTelegraph (Australia) 11 January 2018,

15. Prof. Gillian Triggs, 'Economic Rights of Migrant and Refugee Women' 24 October 2013

16. Plan International Australia video plan.org.au/walklikeawoman

17. Women's Agenda, March 30, 2017 re George Brandis being called a White male

18. Eryk Bagshaw, 'Stale Pale & Male', Sydney Morning Herald, 30 July 2018

19. J.R.R.Tolkien (1892-1973) https://www.goodreads.com/author/quotes/656983.J_R_R_Tolkien

20. Paolo Freire, Pedagogy of the Oppressed,1968

21. Kimberle Crenshaw 'On Intersectionality – Essential Writings 2017

22. Vishen Lakhani in a MindValley Blog on Beckwith's philosophy of awakening, mid-2018

23. Tim Costello, UNSW Gandhi oration, 6 Feb.2019

24. Ken Tanaka YouTube video *https://www.youtube.com/watch?v=crAv5ttax2I* 2013

25. Michael Hing's Documentary 'Where are you really from?' shown on SBS Television Australia https://www.sbs.com.au/guide/article/2018/.../michael-hing-asks-where-are-you-really

26. Paul Krugman, opinion piece in the New York Times Oct. 2, 2018

27. National Geographic 'Race' issue, April 2018

28. Luvvie Ajayi, 8 Feb.2018, https://ideas.ted.com/why-we-need-to-call-out-casual-racism/ - excerpt from her book 'I'm judging you', Henry Holt & Co. 2016,2017

29. Peter Dockrill on Dr. James Watson's views www.sciencealert.com 14 Jan 2019

30. Sasha Sarago writer/director 'Too pretty to be Aboriginal' documentary NITV Australia 8 Jan 2019.

31. Rosalie Kunoth-Monks speech 'I am not the problem' on YouTube, June 10, 2014.

32. Tim Soutphommasane 'On Hate' published February 2019

33. Tom Bathurst, NSW Chief Justice speech at Affinity multicultural foundation dinner Sydney, 2018

34. Katharine Murphy, journalist The Guardian 'The mythology of Meritocracy', 8 Sept. 2018

35. Bonnie Marcus, journalist Chicago Tribune 'The next #MeToo movement: Older women confront ageism', March 20, 2019

36. 'Black Panther' movie, 2018.

37. Jenny Joseph, 2003, poem 'Warning'

38. Rabindranath Tagore, (1861-1941) 'The Champa Flower' poem

39. Ellen Bader & Peter Pearson in The Couples Institute in a newsletter dated 3 March 17

40. Hood, R. 'The Psychology of Religious Fundamentalism' 2005

41. Darcel Rockett for the Chicago Tribune, March 16, 2018 reporting on The National Geographic's Race edition 2018

42. Australian Human Rights Commission Report the *Report on Stolen Children (Bringing them Home 20 years on) published 1997*

Printed in the United States
By Bookmasters